TESTIFYING IN COURT

GUIDELINES *and* MAXIMS
FOR THE EXPERT WITNESS

Stanley L. Brodsky

American Psychological Association
Washington, DC

Fifth printing February 1997

Published by
American Psychological Association
750 First Street, NE
Washington, DC 20002

Copies may be ordered from
APA Order Department
P.O. Box 92984
Washington, DC 20090-2984

In the United Kingdom and Europe, copies may be ordered from
American Psychological Association
3 Henrietta Street
Covent Garden
London WC2E 8LU
England

This book was typeset in ITC Garamond and Adobe Birch by Harper Graphics, Hollywood, MD

Printer: Edwards Brothers, Ann Arbor, MI
Illustrator: Margaret Scott
Designer and Typographer: Shirley Hendricson
Technical/Production Editor: Christine P. Landry

Library of Congress Cataloging-in-Publication Data

Brodsky, Stanley L., 1939–
Testifying in court: guidelines and maxims for the expert witness
    Stanley L. Brodsky.
        p.   cm.
    Includes bibliographical references.
    ISBN 1-55798-128-0 (acid-free paper)
    1. Evidence, Expert—United States.   2. Psychology, Forensic.
I. Title.
KF8965.B76   1991
347.73′67—dc20
[347.30767]   91-16296
                                                                            CIP

Printed in the United States of America

This book is dedicated with love and appreciation
to my sister and my brother:

Barbara Brodsky
and
Howard Brodsky

CONTENTS

Preface

THE IDEA OF WRITING THIS BOOK ABOUT TESTIFYING in court came about in the summer of 1989. While visiting Norman Poythress, I explained that I would like to write a book for expert witnesses but that I did not have an organizing scheme. That is, I had knowledge, experience, and advice, but as a whole it did not hang together enough to let me put it in a book. Norman presented me with a book called *101 Bridge Maxims* (Kelsey, 1983) and told me that I should write the same book for expert witnesses.

101 Bridge Maxims had 101 pages of advice, each of which was summed up in a single one-sentence maxim, or practical principle. I realized instantly that Norman was right and I set out to do for expert witnesses what his book did for bridge players: to discuss common problems followed by useful resolutions and a maxim, all of which would lead to winning testimony in court.

Three names appear frequently in this book: Norman Poythress, who is with the University of South Florida; Tom Grisso, who is with the University of Massachusetts Medical Center; and Stuart Greenberg, who is in private practice in Seattle. I have drawn on their generous advice and have included some of the wonderful stories they have shared with me about their own court experiences.

Two more thank yous are in order. Jay Ziskin has written a series of wide-ranging volumes for attorneys conducting cross-examinations; I have used some of his ideas in my sample questions. Finally, Dena Kirton has been invaluable in helping with the typing of the manuscript.

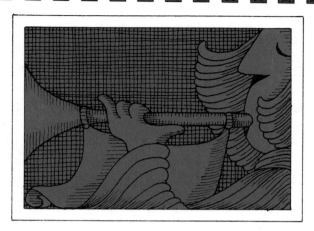

Introduction

FOR THE PAST 20 YEARS I HAVE BEEN LEADING workshops for mental health professionals about testifying in court. What I have learned is that for some potential expert witnesses, the prospect of ever testifying in court is frightening. For other witnesses, a particular kind of case is difficult: sometimes insanity pleas or child custody cases. For still other expert witnesses, testifying is a time of professional mastery, occasionally elation, a chance to explain and defend their knowledge in a public forum.

When witnesses discuss their most terrifying experiences on the stand, some segment of a cross-examination is always described. The themes are similar. The attorney seems to distort the issues or ask questions that inappropriately make small cracks appear to be major faults. These witnesses have related stories of humiliation, distress, and feelings of absolute ineptness.

In similar patterns, witnesses describing their most profoundly satisfying experiences in court also talk about a segment of cross-examination in which the attorney seeks to attack, misrepresent, or embarrass them. What has made the testimony so deeply satisfying has been the witnesses' comfortable competence in handling these attacks. At its best, testifying in court is a time of exhilaration at meeting this intellectual and professional challenge.

My emphasis in this book is in direct response to these dreadful and wonderful experiences on the witness stand. I have focused on the cross-examination process: the questions often asked, the power and control gambits attorneys use, the lines of questions, the nonverbal parrying, and the special limitations of courtroom rules. The basic lessons here are directed at allowing the witness to comply faithfully with the oath of honesty, to be responsive to the questions asked and to the witness role, and to be able to defend oneself, one's opinion, and one's integrity.

No one answer or set of answers can serve for every witness in court, nor is this book a dictionary that provides a definitive response to every cross-examination question. Rather, this book is intended to do one thing: to present a way of thinking about court testimony and to offer a series of choices and alternatives for thinking about testifying in court. My ideas are not necessarily correct or applicable, even for me, in all courtroom situations. My goal is for readers to choose the options that most fit their tastes and style.

If some of these principles and suggestions work, write and let me know. Also let me know if they don't work! Not all of expert mental health testimony is covered here. I have written about what I know. You are invited to write and describe situations that are not covered and that you either have had trouble handling or that you have handled well, and ones that other witnesses might want to hear about. I will credit your name and situation if it is used in the next edition of the book. Please also write me (in care of the following address) if there is anything else you would like to see discussed:

Stanley L. Brodsky
Department of Psychology
P.O. Box 870348
University of Alabama
Tuscaloosa, AL 35487-0348.

❧ 1 ❧

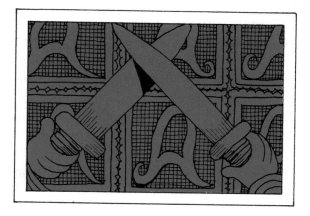

The Admit–Deny

CROSS-EXAMINATIONS SEEK TO REVERSE THE SUBSTANCE OR impact of a witness's testimony. Although this turnaround is attempted in several ways, one of the frequent devices is posing questions to compel the witness to diminish the persuasiveness of his or her opinion. Such questions may examine components of the testimony out of context or they may dwell on marginally relevant issues. For example, in the middle of a cross-examination, the attorney asks, "Isn't it true you psychologists have a long way to go before you really can account for human behavior?" For these and other loaded and unfair efforts to get the witness to confess deficiencies, I suggest use of the admit–deny technique.

The admit–deny answer has two steps. The *admit* step consists of beginning the answer by accurately admitting what has been asked and using a dependent clause. If there is nothing to admit or agree with in the cross-examination question, the admit–deny response should not be used. Instead, a simple correction of fact or opinion should be offered. The admit–deny requires agreement with the truth in some part of the question. A dependent clause is important because the linguistic integrity of the response requires that the attorney wait until a complete sentence or assertion is made before proceeding to the next question. By *dependent clause* I specifically mean beginning a response with the words *although* or *while.* One can also start off with an introductory statement such as "I have two things to say about that" or "that's a complex question."

The second step, the *deny* step, consists of accurately and strongly denying the part of the answer that is untrue by using a closing independent clause. Note that I said *accurately* denying. If no part of the answer calls for a denial, never use a denial. Furthermore, the admit–deny is effective only if the denial is stronger than the admit step.

Let me go back to my illustrative question. The attorney has asked in an aggressive manner, "Isn't it true you psychologists have an awfully long way to go before you really can account for human behavior?"

Some witnesses tend to respond to such loaded questions with a "yes, but" answer. Once a witnesses says "yes, but . . . ." the linguistic demands of allowing the witness to answer have been met, and the attorney can justly cut off the witness with a firm "thank you, you have answered the question."

The *admit* step would be to acknowledge the truth of the question in a dependent clause, such as "Although it is true we psychologists have a long way to go to account for human behavior, ..." Notice that no complete answer is yet given. That incompleteness permits the witness to continue.

If a weak *deny* step is given, the technique has not been successful. Thus, an unconvincing witness would say,

"Although it is true we psychologists have a long way to go to understand human behavior, we are hoping to be able to do so."

This deny segment convinces nobody. In contrast, consider this strong denial:

"Although it is true we psychologists have a long way to go to understand human behavior, we are proud and pleased that we have been able to work toward objective, verifiable, and standardized procedures for understanding and helping people in emotional trouble."

The admit–deny can be especially helpful to a witness who has had an attorney distract the court from the clinical or scientific findings and instead get the witness stuck on polemics or unanswerable queries. In those cases, the *deny* part of the admit–deny can profitably return to the conclusions of the witness. In my example, the witness might respond:

"Although it is true that the field of psychology has a long way to go to fully understand human behavior it is my definite professional opinion, based on a careful and detailed assessment, that Elizabeth flourishes in the care of her mother and she does not with her father."

A shift in control occurs with this response. The witness has gone back to the reason for the testimony. Also, note the slight wording change in the *admit* step. The witness makes it the field of psychology, instead of the more personal "we," and the witness has added the adverb "fully" before "understand" so that the judge and court know that it is the unlikely goal of *fully* understanding human behavior that is so distant.

A word of caution is in order. The admit–deny technique is dynamite. It takes power away from the cross-examining attorney and gives it to the witness. It is both responsive and resistant. However the admit–deny will flop if the witness is seen as evasive. The first part of the answer *must* specifically address the essence of the question. The technique similarly becomes ineffective if overused. The admit–deny then will appear as a shady ploy to escape answering questions rather than as a responsible way of addressing complex issues.

THE MAXIM: *Handle loaded and half-truth questions by first admitting the true part in a dependent clause and then strongly denying the untrue part in an independent clause.*

❧ 2 ❧

Advocacy:
1. The "Bought Expert" Accusation

IF ANY ONE CHARACTERISTIC ALLOWS AN EXPERT TO testify and be believed, it is the presumption of the expert's trustworthiness and impartiality. Training and skills are indicators of an objective, detached professional. Impartiality lends power to the expert witness's testimony and thus is a subject for cross-examination attack. One of the frequent attacks on trustworthiness suggests that the witness is a "bought expert," testifying for the money rather than for substantive reasons.

A national expert on prediction of violence was employed by the defense not too long ago in a suit alleging that a psychiatric hospital had been negligent in releasing a patient who later murdered a companion. This expert was careful and scholarly in his response to the direct examination, and the impact of this part of his testimony was taken even more seriously than it otherwise might have because of his outstanding credentials. The cross-examining attorney decided on the strategy of portraying the witness as a bought expert.

The cross-examination was short and much of it was directed at the witness's fee of $250 an hour. The attorney asked about the hourly fee, the total amount of time billed, the "whopping large" total fee the witness expected to get, and how much less other experts charged for similar tasks. The witness answered the questions with discomfort and without elaboration. The clear message at the end of the cross-examination was that this expert witness was not impartial because of the many thousands of dollars he was receiving. As a consequence, the jury devalued this witness's excellent testimony and found for the opposing side.

My suggestion is to confront the beast. Instead of allowing a protracted series of implications of bias, the witness needs to declare the nature of fees and impartiality, perhaps by saying, "Your question(s) seem to imply that my opinions in this matter are for sale for the price of my fee. Would you like me to address that issue in answering your question?"

In a discussion of this issue, Ames Robey and I (Brodsky & Robey, 1973) have shared one of our preferred replies to these implications of being bought:

> It has been said that "whose bread we eat, his song we sing." It is for exactly that reason I bend over backwards to double and triple check my findings, to insure there is no hint of bias interfering with my conclusions. (p. 176)

This latter statement undermines the cross-examination. Rather than the attorney successfully condemning the witness's objectivity by innuendo, the witness openly addresses the whole concern. The witness's openness and awareness of possible partiality as a result of being hired by one side reduces the power of the questions about this concern.

THE MAXIM: *Respond to implications of being a bought expert by showing awareness of the issue and assertively presenting the foundations of your objectivity.*

❧ 3 ❧

Advocacy: 2. The Pull to Affiliate

BOUGHT EXPERTS MAY OR MAY NOT EXIST, DEPENDING on one's perspective. Those who believe experts can be bought describe individuals who conform their opinions to the side that employs them. Although a few rare birds may indeed be bought, my perspective is that a subtle social–psychological process influences many witnesses toward "our" side. The courtroom drama does have an us-versus-them dichotomy. Just as the attorneys accept the viewpoint of their side, some expert witnesses may do the same. The affiliation process is rarely deliberate or conscious. Instead the pull, and sometimes the reality, is to shape one's opinions in small ways to conform to what is seen as the right side.

Almost all expert witnesses would deny that their opinions are so influenced. However, the affiliation process begins early. From the time the attorney first speaks with a potential expert, the attorney probes, suggests, assures, and woos. If the expert is overly reluctant or resistant, the attorney may rule out the expert as a participant. Sometimes the expert does the ruling out. I was once asked by an attorney to assess both the psychological impact on several women of being assaulted at a rock concert and the degree to which the concert organizers could have prevented the assaults by beefing up the security force on hand. The attorney wanted me to commit myself in advance to a likely finding of catastrophic impact on the women and clear preventive potential by the organizers. His insistence made it clear to me that I wanted no part of these tasks and I withdrew.

As often as I withdraw, I stay with cases—and so do most experts. As the cases progress, a litmus test for continued involvement occurs at the findings stage. The expert reports, usually by telephone, and the attorney decides about using the expert in court. If this decision is positive, then a series of additional stimulus demands to affiliate with this side take place. Meetings occur with the attorney. There is talk about the best way to present the expert's findings and opinions. Discussions may take place about the likely strategy of the opposing attorneys. A meeting prior to deposition may have the attorney helping the expert prepare. It is not unusual to observe an exchange of cooperative actions and warm feelings.

Under these conditions, the impartiality of the expert may be compromised. The expert may want the attorney to win in order that the expert's findings be validated by the judge's or jury's findings. The expert may anticipate a rugged cross-examination, and the consequent anxiety may prompt affiliation with the employing attorney. A natural process of reducing cognitive dissonance can occur in which reservations and uncertainties about the findings fade as the commitment to the case and side become stronger.

These events constitute a far greater hazard to impartiality than the mythical bought witness. Their impact is gradual and beyond the immediate awareness of the expert. These influences are sufficiently powerful that they may be the single greatest threat to expert integrity.

Becoming aware of these events is a first way of preventing them. The expert who is conscious of the unfolding of these influences can recognize and step back from them.

A second way of prevention is to evaluate the degree of emotional and personal commitment to the outcome. If the expert

9

becomes more involved and more certain of the findings *after* the data are gathered and the opinion is first formed, this expert is losing objectivity.

A third and more formal method of examining impartiality at the early stages is to calculate an *objectivity quotient* in which the number of cases in which one agrees with the employing attorney is divided by the total number of cases.[1] If the quotient is high, say .80 or more, the expert may need to examine possible preexisting bias. A more reasonable quotient may be in the .60–.80 range. This calculation needs to be utilized cautiously because sometimes a prescreening is implicit in the nature of the expert's practice or in the base rate of the kinds of legal problems with which the expert deals.

THE MAXIM: *Check and recheck that routine pulls toward affiliation are not diminishing the impartiality of the expert role.*

---

[1]Some years ago I read a proposal that a similar "integrity quotient" be developed for forensic work. The author and source are now long disappeared from memory and files and I have not been able to retrieve them. Thus, I owe acknowledgments for this idea to some unknown author.

❧ 4 ❧

Becoming Current

A FEW YEARS AGO I ATTENDED A MEETING at which a speaker observed that "Psychologists are like the Bourbon Kings; they learn nothing, forget nothing."[1] The wisdom of this cynical remark is how much psychologists and other professionals gain the bulk of their knowledge from their formal education. When they had to learn great amounts of information in graduate school, they did. However, once on their own, many professionals read little, or they depend much more on their experience for knowledge. They stay current in their field in a haphazard manner, reading articles here, attending workshops or seminars there, without an overall plan or conceptualization of what they need to know.

In his writings, Alvin Toffler has argued that the accumulated amount of human knowledge doubles every ten years. This estimate applies equally to the health professions as to most scientific fields.

---

[1]Bob Hoch may have been responsible for this remark. In any case, apologies are extended to the Bourbon Kings: No slight was intended.

Thus, if you completed your formal studies ten years ago, you should have some concerns about how current and accurate that knowledge is now.

A good illustration can be seen in the writings about eyewitness accuracy. In the late 1970s, a flurry of writings and research by Loftus, Yarmey, and others pointed to eyewitness identification as being fallible and unreliable. Many psychologists in criminal cases began testifying to that effect. Then a conference and an article in the *American Psychologist* by McClosky and Egeth (1983) sharply challenged the degree to which the eyewitness research findings could be generalized to the real-world crimes for which individuals were being tried.

One friend of mine was unfamiliar with the McClosky position. Thus, in the late 1980s, when he testified about eyewitness inaccuracy, he was unprepared for cross-examination questions on these issues. His testimony was less effective than it might have been otherwise. When we talked about the difficulties he had on the witness stand, he asked me about the McClosky and Egeth (1983) article and how to respond to these criticisms that were new to him.

My response was to tell him to discuss the controversy but also to point out how McClosky's work had served to prompt a series of studies that eventually made the hypotheses about eyewitness inaccuracy more compelling. Thus, consider an attorney asking,

"Doctor, isn't it true that McClosky has, in your most prestigious journal, established that eyewitness accuracy research is limited and not accurate for cases such as this one?"

The prepared witness could answer,

"We have taken McClosky's criticisms very seriously, and the field has responded with a series of excellent studies to fill just the gaps in knowledge he has identified. We consider his criticisms to have been of great help to us in clarifying the next directions in which our research had to go."

This particular witness response did two important things. It allowed the witness to assume the knowledgeable role of a wise overseer of current developments. It also pointed out that the witness was not an unseeing advocate but an impartial observer.

The principle of staying current is not limited to eyewitness accuracy. Every expert should be a current expert. As a matter of routine, I take time before a court appearance to see what has been happening in the specific subject area about which I will testify. I will read a few reviews or articles. I do not try to review everything because I would be spending my entire waking life reviewing books and chapters. However, I look at the important journals or recent books to learn the new findings and issues. I do not undertake this task simply to defend myself on the witness stand (there are intrinsically good reasons to stay current), but it is a lovely consequence that I feel both a sense of mastery and of being in command when issues of currency and new knowledge come up.

THE MAXIM: *Review current literature on the topic about which you will testify.*

❧ 5 ❧

Burden of Proof and Degree of Certainty

YOUR TESTIMONY HAS BEEN GOING PRETTY WELL. DURING the direct examination, you presented the nature of your observations and data in an organized way and were able to communicate what you wished. Now during the cross-examination, the attorney starts using certain legal terms that make you uncomfortable. The attorney asks, "Were you aware, Doctor, when you conducted your evaluation, that the burden of proof lies with the prosecution?" or "In your routine assessments, do you operate with a presumption of sanity? And do the mental health professions proceed with a presumption of sanity?"

At this point, some witnesses become ill at ease. Legal concepts, such as burdens of proof and presumptions of sanity, have been introduced into mental health or scientific testimony. First, witnesses should know what these basic legal concepts are and second, how to address (or not address) these issues.

Returning to the initial question and assuming that the question is allowed (it would be where I frequently testify), here are some answers: "I conduct my evaluations according to the best existing psychological and clinical standards, and not according to courtroom rules or what the legal professions do." This simple response anticipates a line of questions about the clinician's use of burden of proof and cuts it off. Similar responses would observe that the clinician is not an expert in the law, cannot testify about legal issues, or thinks only about the client and the findings in an evaluation. A witness's initial answer of yes or no can also lead to the above narrative answers in response to follow-up questions by the attorney.

Perhaps the more challenging question that arises from inquiries about awareness of burden of proof is what *standard* of proof the expert has used. Has the expert used a *preponderance of evidence* as the standard of certainty to draw a conclusion? The standard of *clear and compelling evidence?* The standard of *beyond a reasonable doubt?* Some experts have indeed conceptualized their work along such dimensions, and they should share their concepts and standards in their testimony. Most expert witnesses have not thought through their judgments in these legally derived criteria. Indeed, Curran and McGarry (1986) suggested that the application of degrees of certainty "can put severe strain on the ethically responsible professional witness" (p. 531). For them and for me, one of the best pertinent answers would be, "In clinical work, we do not apply these particular criteria. My testimony is based on the criterion of reasonable scientific (or medical or psychological) certainty." Another interchangeable phrase for such answers is, "It is my best professional judgment that is always my criterion for my clinical conclusions."

The "presumption of sanity" question posed earlier may be addressed with these same kinds of answers. Sanity is a legal concept and not a psychological question. Psychological and forensic assessments, the witness may explain, are structured with no such presumptions, but in the operating principle that reasonable psychological certainty of the clinical findings themselves is what is important. I should note that it may be wise not to define in court what is meant by reasonable psychological (or scientific) certainty. When Norman Poythress (1982) decided to define it, he was startled. Here is what he wrote:

> Now in my prior 80–100 court appearances, whenever the phrase 'reasonable psychological certainty' has been used, I've left it to the attorney to ferret the meaning. (They *never* do.) But today, for whatever reason, I was full of ethical zeal! I mean, I was inspired! Geared up! Wired up! Fired up! I decided to show a little initiative, assert myself in the proceedings, and ventured to suggest *sua sponte* (pretty sharp, huh?) that perhaps it would be best if I defined the phrase 'reasonable psychological certainty' so that the jury had some idea of what I meant by it in my opinion testimony to follow.
>
> Well, let me tell you guys, the courtroom turned into Star Trek! . . . it was as if I had fired all lasers at "stun" force, resulting in temporary immobility of all parties, followed by a rather quick recovery in the form of objections from counsel, querilous looks from the bench, and the hasty removal of the jury from the courtroom in a flurry of activity. . . . I had committed the ultimate sacrilege. I had suggested deflowering the immaculate psychologist-in-the-sky who always has opinions based on reasonable psychological (i.e., scientific) certainty. (p. 41)

Eventually, a clarifying and useful discussion emerged in the courtroom, and Norman did take pains to point out that judicial decorum was maintained. The lesson that Norman drew, and that I like, is that clinicians pulling their carts along in the ruts and trenches of legal mental health paths have to be darned careful about deciding what new directions to take.

THE MAXIM: *Burdens of proof and degrees
of defined certainty are legal concepts.
Do not accept, define, or incorporate them into
clinical, psychological, or scientific testimony
(unless you really know what you are doing).*

❧ 6 ❧

Challenges to Experience:
1. Insufficient Experience

O NE OF THE REASONS I HAVE ROUTINELY OFFERED free follow-up consultation to the participants in my expert witness work-shops is that few people ever do follow-up. In this case, however, a nursing consultant did: She sought me out for help in a case coming to trial the next week. Her testimony had been attacked during the deposition and she felt she had not handled the attacks well.

The lawsuit had been filed on behalf of a woman who had died in a nursing home from complications of dicubiti (bedsores). The woman had walked into the nursing home, developed severe bedsores within a week, and died a few months after. The nursing consultant was preparing to testify that unnecessary confinement of the patient in a hospital bed and insufficient turning of the patient proximately caused the bedsores.

During the deposition, the nursing consultant had been chal-lenged on her lack of direct experience. For twenty-five years she had taught and consulted about nursing care, but since completing her nursing training and since well before receiving her PhD, she had not cared for any patients. During the deposition, she had been made to feel embarrassed and ashamed that she had no recent experience with direct care of patients. The opposing attorneys had made her feel that this lack of experience invalidated her opinion, and the nursing consultant said her feeling was reflected in her hesitant statements.

The principle of testimony that applies in this and in all such challenges is to attend to one's true base of expertise. If an attorney makes the witness uncomfortable because of lack of relevant experience, the witness needs to put the matter in perspective. A good attorney can always phrase a question to identify a lack of specific experience. The witness must be attentive to the question but not let the question be personally disruptive. The case that I am discussing will illustrate the process.

The nursing consultant stammered and apologized in the deposition. In our pretrial meetings, she developed these responses to attacks on her insufficient experience:

"I am honored that so many people have seen fit to want my opinion on teaching young nurses and advising nursing homes how to offer good patient care."

"Nurses involved full time in patient care do not often have the time and opportunities I do to visit many settings and to get an overview of the issues and dilemmas in nursing care."

"The nature of nursing, like most professions, is that a large number of people are involved in direct service, a small number are their immediate supervisors, and a still smaller number of us are in the role of consultants to and evaluators of these direct care and supervisory professionals."

"It is not necessary for me to turn patients in their beds daily for several years to understand exactly how dicubiti are caused and prevented, and how they could have been prevented in this case."

With these thoughts in mind, the nursing consultant was poised in the cross-examination in court. She was not distressed by attacks on her limited practical experience and instead kept to the salient issue of her actual expertise that had brought her to the courtroom.

THE MAXIM: *When challenged about insufficient experience, keep track of the true sources of your expertise.*

❦ 7 ❧

Challenges to Experience:
2. Irrelevant Experience

NO MATTER HOW MUCH PROFESSIONAL OR SCIENTIFIC EXPERIENCE an expert witness has had, a well-prepared cross-examining attorney can always challenge its applications to the case at hand. The attorney's flow of questions will be directed toward the kinds of first-hand experience that the expert has *not* had. If the attorney is successful, the judge or jury will believe that the experienced witness does not have sufficient expertise about the particular client, problem, locale, or issue.

With jury trials, in rural areas, or when the case is otherwise weak, the opposing attorney may bring up the often irrelevant experience issue of the witness's possible ignorance of the local venue. Some attorneys elicit a long string of admissions designed to portray the expert as an uninformed outsider. This line of questions proceeds as follows:

"You weren't born here in Jefferson County, were you Doctor?"

"You weren't raised here in Jefferson County, were you?"

"You didn't go to grade school here in Jefferson County?"

"Your children didn't go to grade school here in Jefferson County?"

"You don't know first hand what it is like for a child to be raised and educated here in Jefferson County, do you?"

"In fact, isn't it fair to say that there is a huge amount you do not know personally about Jefferson County living, values, beliefs, and education?"

Although this example addresses a county in which the expert does not live, the questioning can readily address a state, community, neighborhood, racial or ethnic group experiences, religious outlooks, and any other demographic divider. The witness can be brought to acknowledge the personal absence of Hispanic (or any other) experience.

Witnesses have many acceptable ways of responding. Some witnesses will answer briefly and nondefensively, without attempting to interject statements of their own. Some witnesses will use the push–pull or admit–deny replies discussed elsewhere. Other witnesses choose to correct a potential impression that they are not expert with this individual client. They explain about common elements in personality. They discuss the ways in which they do explore cultural influences. They go beyond the narrow question and answer the overarching question about their lack of relevant expertise by accurately pointing out what they do and do not know about this type of client.

Occasionally, attorneys who see no other path to courtroom effectiveness carry this line of questions to near-absurd extremes. Such attorneys may ask questions of this ilk:

"Just how many Native American women from Vermont accused of murdering their children have you evaluated?" "What? Not even one before this case?" "Not even *one* at any time in your career?"

The witness might answer by pointing out the base rate, that virtually nobody else has evaluated somebody like this either, and that certain principles of assessment and scientific knowledge are designed to be generalizable across very different individuals. As in all such questions, the witness should straightforwardly present any limitations that do exist with diverse populations. However, the foundations for working with the population at hand should also be presented.

THE MAXIM: *Be prepared to present the bases for generalizability of findings and demographic communalities in your testimony.*

❧ 8 ❧

Challenges to Experience:
3. The Case Against Experience

S OME ATTORNEYS TAKE THE TIME TO PREPARE WELL and will use a
series of questions designed to discredit the value of professional
experience of any sort. Such questions, which have been especially
well developed by Ziskin and Faust (1988), confront the witness
with selected research findings that have concluded that psychology
graduate students and other professionals in training are just as adept
in psychotherapy and in psychodiagnostic work as senior, creden-
tialed, experienced professionals. Naturally, this argument is mobi-
lized only with witnesses with much experience. This issue is absent
with new professionals or professionals in training, on the witness
stand, who essentially are asked what makes them think they are
competent after so little experience. The questions put to experienced professionals follow this pattern:

"Is there any substantiated scientific reason to believe that
professional experience is associated with increased competence?"

"In fact, isn't it true that a series of scientific investigations
have concluded that people with years of experience like yours are

no better than untrained, unlicensed students and laypeople in assessing and treating clients?"

"Can you describe even one published scholarly report to support the belief that the sorts of experiences you have had are at all related to knowledge or skills?"

If the attorney has read the Ziskin and Faust (1988) volumes, these questions will be accompanied by specific citations of articles. Those citations appear in learned treatise questions that begin with a question about whether the witness is familiar with the study by Smith and Jones, which produced negative findings for experience.

The witness in such a cross-examination should know, first of all, that the attorney's sources are selectively one-sided. Although it is easy to feel overwhelmed by repeated citations of studies that imply little competence from experience, the witness needs to understand that a series of more recent studies have contradicted these earlier reports. Knowing the literature is the best defense. Almost as important, the witness should continue to hold faithfully to what he or she believes about the value of personal experience. The witness also needs to affirm the foundations of those beliefs in the testimony. The following are some sample replies to this challenge:

"While a series of pro and con articles about experience have appeared, my reading of the literature is that the commonsense notion that experience is important has been supported."

"I cannot speak for anyone else's experience, but my own professional experiences have exposed me to many different kinds of clients and situations, and these experiences have been invaluable in understanding human behavior."

"Nobody has studied my experience. Indeed, it is not the nature of scientific study to look at individuals' experience."

"We are happy that those of us involved in training and in the field have been able to contribute enough to help today's students to a high level of competence. However, I doubt that any of our students or experienced professionals would agree with your statement about students being as good as experienced staff. The people who conduct such studies tend to work with artificial situations, with clients who are hypothetical, and do not understand what the state of current professional work actually is."

Faced with these responses, most attorneys beat a hasty departure from this topic. A few attorneys will stubbornly pursue the same questions further. The witness should be equally stubborn in asserting genuinely felt confidence in the value of professional experience.

THE MAXIM: *Challenges to professional experience should be met with a knowledge of the literature and affirmations of the worth of your own experience.*

❧ 9 ❧

Changing Your Mind

WHAT WITNESSES WANT IS TO BE HONEST, TO be effective, and to be well received. Most of the time, witnesses are able to accomplish these three goals. Sometimes, however, issues are brought up during the cross-examination that make it difficult for witnesses to be all of those things.

One such influence is what the ambitious cross-examining attorney seeks: for the witnesses to change their minds. All expert witnesses who testify often enough will run into situations in which there is enormous pressure to change their minds about some important aspects of their testimony. Many sources of such pressure exist, including hypothetical questions, the presentation of information that conflicts with the witnesses' findings, and the exposure of areas of scientific ignorance or incompleteness in the assessment procedures.

When led through these areas, some witnesses retract the essential inferences from their work. To my way of thinking, these retractions are always wrong. The findings of expert witnesses should lie in their scientific or professional work. If the case is a matter of child custody, the decision should be drawn from the interviews and tests of parents and child and how these results fit with existing scholarly information. If the case is an assessment of criminal responsibility, then the source for such conclusions should similarly be in the clinical interviews, behavioral observations, history, psychopathology, and reconstruction in time of the target behaviors and person. Conclusions should neither be produced nor changed by cross-examinations.

This rule is fundamental: *Do not change conclusions on the witness stand.*

Ah, but suppose the questions are so probing that as a witness you feel that you have been negligent and have not done something you should have? Under these circumstances, you need to remember two things. First, remember that challenging information presented in the form of cross-examination questions is always suspect. That is, if you are asked about a client's behavior as described by a prior witness, the description will have been selectively presented according to the attorney's needs in the case. Second, remember where the conclusions actually developed. A few challenging questions that reveal flaws, say, in the information-gathering procedures, can make witnesses lose track of all of the truly meaningful work that originally led to their conclusions. At these times, try to return to those original data and procedures. Here is that kind of response:

"Based on the full evaluation I conducted with Miss Jones this past June, and based on the five hours of interviewing and full review of her social history, and based on my eleven years of clinical experience, it is my considered judgment that she was not in control of her behavior or herself at the time of the killing."

If the attorney pushes further with questions that present new information to you, it is okay to delineate the boundaries of your information. You can always indicate that your conclusions were based only on these interviews and data. If the attorney presents conflicting information, stay with your conclusions, but when pressed with genuine concerns (as opposed to lawyers' ploys), it is ultimately acceptable to state that you can return and evaluate Miss Jones further in light of possible new information. Nevertheless, you should emphasize that you stay with your opinion that came from the evaluation you have already conducted.

THE MAXIM: *Do not change a professional opinion on the basis of a cross-examination. Your opinions should always arise from your data.*

❧ 10 ❧

Child Sexual Abuse:
1. Lying and Fantasy

MOST EXPERT WITNESSES IN CHILD SEXUAL ABUSE CASES testify for the prosecution, usually reporting the results of interviews with the child. Although there are no good base-rate data about how accurate appraisals of abuse are, one estimate is that less than five percent of all allegations are false (Jones & McGraw, 1987). The present guidelines are directed at the expert witness who has assessed an incident of child sexual abuse and who is being cross-examined by the defense attorney about the degree to which lying or fantasies by the child may have produced the report of abuse. These principles have been discussed in more detail elsewhere (Hovey & Brodsky, 1990). The cross-examination questions may include the following queries:

"Isn't it true that all children lie at times?"

At this point many witnesses get wary and defensive. A fine, nondefensive answer is "Yes. Absolutely! All adults too." This answer uses the push–pull principle and shows an understanding of the overall problem of lying. The attorney may well pursue this inquiry further, in which case the witness might observe that children typically lie to get out of trouble ("Mary did it. I didn't.") rather than to get into trouble, which is the functional result of allegations of sexual abuse. Suppose the attorney asks:

"Isn't it true that Judy (the child) is a known liar?"

If this is new information to the witness, that should be stated. If the witness has heard this about Judy before, the response might draw on how clinical assessments by experienced clinicians are all the more important, just to be able to sort out truths from falsehoods.

"Isn't it possible for lies to become set in concrete as a child repeats them, so that the child really begins to believe them?"

Again, a simple "of course it is possible" may suffice, as well as an observation that this process occurs for children and adults alike. Assuming that the witness has considered and rejected this issue in the evaluation, a discussion is in order of factors that contradict the lies-poured-in-concrete hypothesis, along with what would have supported the hypothesis. Thus, clinical data possibly would have included the child's spontaneity, the sexual knowledge that is not age-appropriate, and the absence of a rigid retelling of the incident from rote memory.

"Don't young children have active fantasy lives?" ("Yes, often.") "Isn't it entirely possible that this accusation of sexual abuse is nothing more than wishful thinking or fantasy triggered by a sexual scene in a television show, or in a video, or from a playmate's description of abuse?"

This scenario is an unlikely possible interpretation. Wishful thinking and fantasies are oriented toward positive experiences. Few children or adults fantasize about being assaulted. Wishful thinking is directed toward solving problems rather than imagining or creating them, which, I have noted, is what happens when an allegation is made.

"What do actuarial studies show about the frequency of sexual fantasies and abuse in children?"

This question is usually a shot in the dark to get the witness to admit ignorance of actuarial studies. It is certainly acceptable to do just that, but it is also okay to go back to the evaluation of the child at hand and report what was found about the nature of her or his fantasies and how they fit with the overall clinical picture.

These cross-examination questions are intended to portray the witness as unthinkingly and uncritically accepting the child's allegations as part of an antidefendant bias. The critical judgments used in child abuse evaluations are important to emphasize in reply. An additional helpful comment on objectivity can be about the many cases of alleged child abuse that the witness has not found supported and that never come to court.

THE MAXIM: *Questions about children's lying and fantasies should be answered with open acknowledgment of their existence and the ways in which the clinical examination ruled them out as causes of the allegations of abuse.*

❧ 11 ❧

Child Sexual Abuse:
2. Anatomically Detailed Dolls

AS A MATTER OF COURSE, EXPERT WITNESSES SHOULD be prepared to testify about any of the foundations of their work. However, extensive preparation is particularly called for in the case of issues that are in the media or about which controversy is boiling. An example of an issue that meets both of these extensive preparation criteria is the use of anatomically detailed dolls in evaluations of child sexual abuse. Nationally publicized cases of alleged child abuse have highlighted problems in the use of such dolls. Furthermore, issues have been raised about normative responses to the dolls in nonabused children, whether the dolls stimulate sexual fantasies, and whether the questions asked serve to shape the children's answers. Sources of useful information on the topic include Boat and Everson (1988); Goodman and Aman (1990); Jampole and Weber (1987); Sivian, Schor, Koeppl, and Noble (1988); and White and Santilli (1988). Drawing on the controversial issues, a well-read attorney may ask questions similar to the following ones during cross-examination:

"Why are standardization and norms important in clinical assessment of children?" (The answer would address the need for known, verifiable structures for evaluation.)

"Isn't it correct that many different anatomically detailed dolls are manufactured?" (Yes.)

"And isn't it true that how much anatomical detail in the dolls, in their design, size, and sexual nature, differ widely from one manufacturer to another?" (The answer is yes.) At this point the witness may be aware that the attorney has prepared carefully.

"Would you please tell this court if anywhere in this country published and accepted standardized procedures exist for using anatomically detailed dolls for weighing reports of abuse or for interviews aided by use of anatomically detailed dolls?"

This question allows the witness the option of acquiescing and simply saying "there are none" or "I don't know" or choosing the alternative of providing a narrative answer. One narrative, powerful answer might be,

"No. It is just for that reason that standardized procedures are not available that interviews using anatomically detailed dolls call for experienced, trained clinicians who know how to be objective and who have developed substantial practical norms."

The attorney might persist by presenting the witness with a copy of the relevant written documents and asking (accurately):

"Isn't it true that major committees and boards of the American Psychological Association have concluded that these dolls cannot be considered standardized assessment tools and that use of the dolls does not conform to professional standards for educational and psychological tests?"

This area of questioning might also ask if the witness is familiar with various expert sources who have criticized these dolls as inaccurate, invalid devices that lead to false conclusions of child sexual abuse. The prepared witness knows both the criticisms and the responses in the research and professional literature. Thus, the witness might reply that the statement written in 1990 by the American Psychological Association's (APA's) Committee on Children,

Youth, and Families and the Committee on Psychological Tests and Assessment and approved by the APA Council of Representatives in 1991 not only made the comments noted but also concluded that doll-centered assessments may be the best available, practical solutions in the hands of competent psychologists. Competence, incidently, was defined in part as experience, knowledge of the clinical and empirical rationales, and careful documentation of the procedures used, including videotaping when possible.

THE MAXIM: *In the controversial area of anatomically detailed dolls in the assessment of child sexual abuse, witnesses should know both the criticisms and supporting data, as well as the requisite professional competencies that accompany their use.*

❧ 12 ❧

Client Dissimulation:
1. Clinical Considerations

ISSUES THAT BRING MENTAL HEALTH PROFESSIONALS TO COURT often mean that the clients have motives for creating an impression of being more disturbed or healthier than they are. Clients who are hoping that an evaluation will lead them to be found not competent to stand trial or not criminally responsible may simulate emotional disturbance. Clients who are being evaluated as part of a personal injury action or for workman's compensation similarly may be moved to overstate their display of distress or disabilities.

On the other side are clients who want to appear better than they are, to exaggerate their existing signs of health. Clients are so motivated at presentence evaluations and at evaluations that precede parole hearings or release decisions from involuntary commitment. Clients wish to be positively assessed for employment or admission to a program that selects in part on the basis of psychological well-being.

For the purposes of this discussion, I use the customary label of these motives, that is, as the inclination to "fake bad" or "fake good." Unfortunately, the term *fake* hints of illicit or manipulative motivations. My position is that the desire to achieve a goal that is reasonable by all social criteria, such as avoiding a long prison sentence, getting a large financial award, or getting out of a psychiatric hospital, is altogether legitimate. These efforts at impression management should not by themselves elicit in the clinician any automatic assignment of a psychopathological label such as personality disorder.

Whether the motive is to fake bad or fake good, the responsibility of the clinician is to consider such motives and their possible effects in assessment and testimony. Many techniques exist for detecting this type of impression management. The book, *Telling Lies: Clues to Deceit in the Marketplace, Politics, and Marriage*, by Paul Ekman (1985) is an excellent source of research information on nonverbal indicators of interpersonal deceit. Within most clinical interviews and tests, inconsistency in results and self-presentation yield relevant information about faking.

Even the most conscientious and thorough clinician may be presented with cross-examination questions about aspects of faking by clients. Being prepared for the overall issue is a first step of defense against aggressive questioning in this area. Consider some real-life questions that have been asked in cross-examinations:

"What standardized tests did you use to determine possible faking by Mr. Smith?"

"Can you be fooled, Doctor?"

"Is it possible for a psychologist to be so fooled that the psychologist doesn't know it happened?"

"Can individuals selectively show one or another particular aspect of their personalities, according to the situations they are in?"

One way of handling such questions is to follow the implied line of logic and answer the essential issue. A witness may choose to answer as I did one day when an attorney asked me the first of those questions. I responded as follows:

"Every time I do a court evaluation I consider the issue of

possible faking. I would be professionally remiss if I did not. Faking can be observed in a half dozen ways during an evaluation."

The attorney asked me what were these half dozen ways. He should not have. I described the nature of normative information in the interviews and tests I had used. I spoke about my own experience. I talked of how clinicians are trained to withhold even minor hints of "correct" answers. I commented on the meaning of discrepancies between verbal and nonverbal behaviors. I explained how clients' tones of voice and facial expressions are revealing. I noted the differences between clients wanting to make a particular impression and succeeding in making that impression. I elaborated on the differences between judgments that a layperson would make and judgments a trained professional makes.

The same strategy applies to the remaining questions, which can be answered in this vein:

"Although any clinician potentially can be fooled, the clinical data are so strong and clear that little if any likelihood exists that Mr. Smith fooled me when I assessed him."

"Of course, in every social situation, individuals do selectively show particular aspects of their personalities. It is for that reason we use standard procedures that permit us to take these tendencies into account."

These replies have in common a compelling restatement of the validity and sensitivity of clinical evaluations. The witnesses who keep these foundations in mind will be better equipped to handle questions about client dissimulation.

THE MAXIM: *Challenges about clients faking bad or faking good should be met with affirmative statements of clinical validity, sensitivity, and vigilance for client dissimulation.*

❦ 13 ❦

Client Dissimulation:
2. Research Considerations

NOW THAT THE CLINICAL ISSUES IN TESTIMONY ABOUT client dissimulation have been considered, I discuss research findings and testimony. Many useful sources are available, including the cautionary findings of Richard Rogers (1984; Rogers, Harris, & Wasyliw, 1983; Rogers, Turner, Helfield, & Dickens, 1988) suggesting weak scientific and conceptual foundations for detecting malingering. The review by Mendelson (1988) is particularly useful, and I have drawn on it in this discussion.

1. No consensus of clinical opinion exists about base rates of dissimulation. The reliability of clinical judgments about faking is lower than most practitioners would estimate. Furthermore, for some clinicians the moral condemnation involved in "discovering" dissimulation may substantially diminish their objectivity.
2. Neither the standardized nor special faking and malingering scales on objective personality tests yield powerful or unequivocal conclusions about clients faking good or bad. For

example, obvious versus subtle measures, validity scales, and malingering scales on the Minnesota Multiphasic Personality Inventory (MMPI) are not dependably accurate.

3. Selected studies have shown that standardized measures can detect the differences between non-brain-injured individuals simulating brain injury compared with actual brain-injured patients and between actual and faked hearing losses.

4. The initial promise of the Conscious Exaggeration Scale to detect malingering of pain and disability has had equivocal results in continued study. Thus, in personal-injury suits, it should be applied with care and in combination with other assessment measures.

The attorney knowledgeable about these findings may cross-examine with questions such as the following:

"Doesn't the vast scientific literature indicate that clinicians are nowhere near as good as they think they are in detecting malingering?"

The witness aware of the literature might respond that responsible clinicians should pay careful attention to the research findings on malingering and then elaborate on the answer. The witness less aware of research should say honestly that he or she does not know of any vast literature. A follow-up or related question might be,

"What precautions does the research literature specifically support in terms of evaluating people who may be faking disability or personal injury?"

The answer that "I'm not a researcher" may be adequate, but it is nowhere as satisfactory as replying that the literature suggests to do just as the witness has done, which is to be neither overly skeptical nor suggestible and instead apply the best techniques in use. A good attorney would inquire next about exactly which research studies on malingering have supported the techniques used. At this point, the witness needs to either cite studies or retreat to speaking of common and accepted practices in a field that has substantial research foundations.

"What have been the major criticisms of the ways people have tried to study malingering and dissimulation?" After an answer, the next question may be,

"Would you disagree with the assertion that having normal individuals pretend they are disturbed or disabled has been an ineffective and flawed research method of finding out about patterns of dissimulation?"

Several options for responding are available. The push–pull reply would be, "Of course I would not disagree!" An admit–deny would be, "While I surely agree about the weaknesses of those studies, my findings deal with quite different dimensions and are based on clinical work with Ms. Smith." Finally, the witness who is current on research can essentially take over at this time by discoursing about the different methodological strategies, their pros and cons, and implications in the study of dissimulation. By itself, that scares most attorneys away from pursuing this topic further and sends them back to their seats, muttering to themselves about remembering to ask questions only when they know what the answers will be.

THE MAXIM: *Research on client dissimulation should be known and used in clinical work and testimony. Enough of the research findings are equivocal that caution in evaluations and witness statements are always in order.*

❧ 14 ❧

Collaborative Criticism

NOW AND THEN ONE RUNS INTO A TECHNIQUE of cross-examination that is so potent that most experts have difficulty with it. One such powerful technique has been called "collaborative criticism" by a practicing clinician, an attorney, and myself (Greenberg, Feldman, & Brodsky, 1987). The essence of this approach is that the expert witness involuntarily joins the attorney in a critical evaluation of the expert's own discipline and present work.

The attorneys eliciting collaborative criticism often begin by asking about problems in the discipline or profession. The attorneys may ask specifically what criticisms have been leveled by scientists toward clinical practice. Then questions follow about areas of scientific studies that dispute ordinary interviewing procedures. Next, the witnesses may be requested to discuss, in turn, flaws, criticisms, and deficits in the experts' credentials, procedures, and clinical results. If the witnesses attempt to present positive aspects, they are reminded to return to the questions asked about flaws, criticisms, and deficits.

Here are some sample questions:

"In what way is your field lacking in definitive applicable studies that would have assisted you in the methods you employed in the evaluation and in the conclusions you drew from your investigation?"

"Which additional tests would you like to have had an opportunity to administer and which persons would you have preferred to have had more time to interview?"

"Were there additional people you would have wished to interview? Why?"

"Are there additional environments or contexts in which you would have preferred to observe anyone in this evaluation? Why?"

"Doctor, in general, would you please tell this court the important ways in which you think a psychological or psychiatric evaluation might not be an accurate long-term estimate of the kind of person that this individual is?"

"Doctor, you have reported that the father is emotionally suited to be the primary caretaker and parent of this child. Would you please describe for the court the concerns you have or the weakness that you noted in the father's psychological status" (Greenberg et al., 1987, pp. 23, 28).

When this approach works, the attorney impresses the jury or judge with a nonconfrontive, often gentle series of questions. The expert witnesses deliver what may be a devastating critique of their work and fields, without the reservations that would put the matter in some balanced overview.

Some expert witnesses cope by denying weaknesses. Such denials may be satisfactory in response to a few questions. However, the repetitive, absolute denial of flaws makes witnesses appear dogmatic and adversarial. Furthermore, these denials of flaws often are cover-ups of ignorance or of an unwillingness to be self-critical. The ethical responses are to confess ignorance and to be honestly self-critical.

How, in the light of the power of this technique, can conscientious witnesses respond? A first answer is to give the attorneys what they are entitled to. Expert witnesses cannot always come out on top. Nevertheless, witnesses should remember to be poised, confident, and not to treat the questions as unsettling. A matter-of-fact attitude by witnesses will promote matter-of-fact interpretations by the jury or judge.

Finally, witnesses should look for opportunities to take control; that is, they ought to wait for questions that will permit the issues to be put in perspective. Weaknesses and deficits should be correctly identified, but strengths and state-of-the-profession knowledge should be presented as well. Of course, the attorneys will resist. However, once witnesses get the floor, they can use it to describe how weaknesses have been considered, and compensated for, and why their conclusions are valid and meaningful.

THE MAXIM: *Criticize your field as requested, but be poised and matter of fact and look for opportunities to regain control.*

❦ 15 ❦

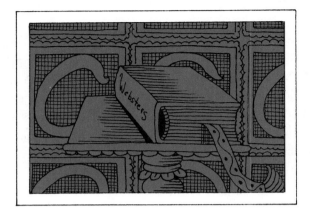

Concepts and Definitions

THE GOOD ATTORNEY WILL ASK THE MEANING OF professional and
scholarly terms. These requests for definitions may occur during
the early meetings between the attorney and witness, during the
direct examination, or by the opposing attorney during the cross-
examination. The absence of such inquiries should be more a source
of concern than their presence. Even knowledgeable and experienced attorneys should inquire about how this particular expert
understands the subject at hand. Witnesses can check out their own
depth of understanding by attempting to answer the question, "Can
I describe the theoretical and scientific foundations that would allow
me to make this kind of statement?" Try these examples.

"This form of depression is long-lasting and will continue to
interfere with his ability to work."

"Would you please describe the theoretical and scientific
foundations of work abilities that would allow a clinician to make
that kind of statement?"

"When five scales on the MMPI are very elevated, this is a
positive sign of severe disturbance."

"Would you describe the theoretical and scientific foundations of the MMPI that would allow a clinician to make that particular statement?"

"I am very confident about my conclusions."

"Would you describe the theoretical and scientific foundations that would support a clinician having that kind of confidence in his or her conclusions?"

"There is very little success in the efforts of clients to fool forensic examiners."

"Would you describe the theoretical and scientific foundations that would allow you to make that kind of statement?"

The same nature of specialized fields that entitles individuals to be qualified as expert witnesses also requires that expert witnesses simplify terms and concepts, as these experts comprehend and use them, for attorneys, judges, and juries. Yet, many witnesses do not distinguish between standard definitions and deeper underlying understandings.

This principle was illustrated by Law Professor Robert M. Lloyd (1989) in his article, "Zen and the Art of Contract Formation," which appeared in the *Journal of Legal Education*. Lloyd put it this way in discussing Supreme Court decisions:

> It is said that a work, because it is "pornography," is not protected by the First Amendment. But to call something pornography is to state the conclusion, not the reason. It is no secret that what the court really does is to look at the work and determine whether it is entitled to First Amendment protection. If it is not, the courts call it "pornography." Justice Stewart was roundly criticized for saying that although he might not be able to define pornography, "I know it when I see it." But it was his critics who showed their lack of understanding, for a definition is not a prerequisite for understanding. And it is surely not a substitute. (pp. 186–187)

I often hear experts using definitions as if they are both the substance of a concept and the conclusion. This process is nowhere more clear than in diagnostic definitions from the American Psychiatric Association's (1987) revised third edition of the *Diagnostic and Statistical Manual of Mental Disorders (DSM-III-R)*. The *DSM-III-R* is deliberately atheoretical and uses a given incidence of specific behaviors as the basis for diagnoses. Mental health expert witnesses often cite the degree to which behaviors meet the criteria as both explanation and conclusion.

What is wrong with this? To begin with, the concepts themselves as described in the *DSM* are often fuzzy. Lists of criteria, three or five of which must be present to affirm the presence of the disorder, gloss over the underlying vagueness with a veneer of objectivity. Even if one can find agreement in the diagnosis of a client, that does not mean that the disorder exists or that these criteria define it. Many clinicians believe that if a diagnostic entity is present in the *DSM*, then it is a true syndrome. The essence of the problem is when witnesses conclude that a disorder is present, and, then, that conclusion is the essence of the testimony. There are alternatives.

A minimum alternative is to look at the foundations of the diagnostic categories. As difficult a task as this seems, reconstructing the ways in which disorders were constructed allows a knowledgeable overview. Suppose, in a trial of an accused child molester, an attorney asks, "Doctor, what is pedophilia?"

The correct *DSM* definition as an answer is, "Pedophilia occurs when a person at least 16 years old has intense sexual fantasies and urges involving sexual activity with a child that recur over at least six months."

Suppose the attorney has listened well and asks a version of "How do you know that?" in the form of

"How did the period of six months become determined?"

"If the urge recurs just twice over a six month period, does that qualify as pedophilia?"

"What are the points in a person's life that turn him or her to pedophilia?"

To these questions, the witness may be well advised to note

the limits of the *DSM*. I suggest answering the first of the questions by observing that six months is used simply to indicate that passing urges or single events are not pedophilia and that five or seven months would have been equally appropriate. The witness might go on to answer the second question by describing how pedophilia has components that fall on a continuum, rather than being an either–or outcome, and that many clients have varying amounts of sexual urges and behaviors toward children. The last question has many answers, including, "Nobody really knows," and "a felt inability to relate sexually to adults."

These in-depth questions are particularly challenging. Although elsewhere in this book I describe many attorney game-playing gambits, this questioning of concepts is serious and deserves a well-considered answer. A useful practice exercise for witnesses is to rehearse testimony with colleagues, who can pose difficult questions repeatedly and help the witness think through the answers.

THE MAXIM: *Good definitions are*
necessary but not sufficient bases
for answering fundamental questions.
Broader conceptual understanding is needed.

❧ 16 ❧

Courtroom as Place Identity

A PLACE IDENTITY DESCRIBES SOME PHYSICAL LOCATION THAT captures some piece of who we are. For most of us, our place identities include our homes and usually offices, places that bring out the feeling "this is me" or "this is mine" or "this place is where I belong."

In the original "Saturday Night Live" television shows, a regular feature was the Coneheads, a family of extraterrestrials living in Middle America. The Coneheads spoke peculiarly, talking of "mass consumables" instead of food. They drank six-packs of beer with all six cans opened, all still linked together, so beer dribbled down their bodies. The Coneheads also had prominent, bald cone-shaped heads rising a foot in the air. All of the Coneheads's neighbors knew the Coneheads did not belong, that is, did not share a common place identity. The strange-looking, strange-talking, strange-eating Coneheads wanted to assume a closer identification with their place of residence, so when puzzled neighbors asked "Where are you from, anyway?", the Coneheads replied "France," and the neighbors were satisfied.

In the same sense, a woman from India I know worked at a psychiatric hospital in Ohio. The patients, puzzled by her strong

South Indian (Madras-British) accent, would ask where she was from. She would reply, "West Virginia," and the patients would be satisfied.

Both of these examples are instructive because they illustrate individuals who are not part of a physical location but who want the comfort and belongingness of such a place identity. Hank Lazer (1989) called those with such partial identities "intellectual boat people," physically present but not part of their culture.

So it is with the new or infrequent witnesses in the courtroom. Although the court is home to others, for the new witness it is a place of discomfort and unfamiliarity. The absence of place identity is seen when the witness privately thinks "I don't belong here" or "What am I doing here?" Lawyers, judges, court reporters, bailiffs, and newspaper reporters all seem to feel at home in the courtroom.

Feeling at home affects how well one performs. The feeling of being in an alien, puzzling place in which a foreign language is spoken or at least where indecipherable phrases are bandied about raises anxiety. If anxiety is high enough, performance diminishes—a lot.

The resolution is to arrange small visits for identification with the courtroom as a physical place and as a staging place. Simple physical presence in the courtroom will help. A law of proximity operates. We like people and places we are often near and that are familiar (everything else being equal). That is why childhood neighbors become good friends or sweethearts.

The new or infrequent witness should go into the empty courtroom alone and sit for awhile. The witness should sit in on other trials to feel more at home. The witness should ask for a waiver of the rule that excludes him or her from observing earlier testimony; most judges are agreeable to the wavier for expert witnesses. Observing the participants in the trial at hand and hearing other experts typically reduces the sense of alienation. Occasionally as an observer, you may become so fed up with the ineptness of other witnesses and the attorneys that you will become eager to get on the witness stand yourself.

THE MAXIM: *Witnesses often feel like aliens in the courtroom: The solution is to be present often and to develop a sense of place identity.*

Credentialing: 1. Facts

"**H**AVE YOU GOT YOUR QUESTIONS?" THE ATTORNEY ASKED me at the beginning of the pretrial meeting.

"What questions do you have in mind?" I wanted to find out.

"You know, the questions I should ask you during the direct examination."

I did not have a list of *all* of the questions he would ask me, although we jointly generated that list quickly. However, I do have a list of standard questions for credentialing me as an expert witness. The questions are not unique to my credentials, and indeed other sources of similar questions have been published (e.g., Macdonald, 1969). The usefulness of having standard questions for the attorney is that complete coverage of one's background and qualifications is ensured. Acceptance as an expert witness by the court is likely to follow more easily.

Here are a set of such questions, which should be modified according to the individual witness's special qualifications:

- Education: Where, when, what degrees, specialties, relevant courses, postdegree formal education;

- Employment: What positions, what level or rank, what responsibilities, when and for how long, current position;
- Licensure or certifications;
- Memberships in professional or scientific societies: At what level, for how long, offices held;
- Honors, awards, and recognitions;
- Publications and presentations: Articles, chapters, books, talks, editorships;
- Grants: Subjects of study, source of funding, amount, how long, results;
- Skills: From workshops, supervision, postdegree training;
- Consultantships;
- Speciality knowledge: Of what methods, clientele, topics, how acquired;
- Experience: What kind, what populations, what role, how relevant to court case.

Two cautions are in order. If the witness does not have any honors, for instance, then the honors item should be deleted. In other words, only actual achievements should be presented. The absence of achievements should not be elicited during the direct examination unless you anticipate cross-examination on the lack of a particular achievement (e.g., knowing that a rebuttal witness is a diplomate).

The second caution is to proffer only items about which one is expert. A witness who had a course in biological bases of human behavior ten years earlier and who never again studied or encountered the subject should not have that course included in the credentialing. The consequences in terms of cross-examination questions about that subject could be awkward. However, if the witness is asked questions about a topic in which the witness's knowledge is minimal or out of date, I suggest an answer such as the following:

"If I gave the impression that I have special expertise on the biological bases of human behavior, I must correct that. My knowledge is primarily from a course I took ten years ago. Actually, my knowledge is much more directed toward assessment of children who have been abused, our concern with Mary in court today."

Stuart Greenberg has suggested to me (and I agree) that for

more seasoned and experienced witnesses, an open-ended approach is a preferred alternative. For example,

Q: "Doctor, is it true that you have been through the process of being qualified as an expert many times before?"

A: "Yes it is."

Q: "Using that experience as a guide, would you please tell this court about your educational background?"

Q: "Your primary employments and professional appointments?"

Q: "Your honors and awards?"

Q: "Your licensure and practice?"

Q: "Your particular expertise in the matter before the court today?"

THE MAXIM: *Prepare a list of professionally relevant and complete qualifying questions for the attorney to use in the opening of the direct examination.*

❧ 18 ❧

Credentialing: 2. Challenges

WHEN I ASKED IF ANYBODY IN THE AUDIENCE feared something in particular during testimony, a tall, soft-spoken man in his forties stood and described his persistent fear. He had been working as a social worker for three years. Everything he learned he had learned on the job. He was afraid of having to defend his education—a BA in history twenty years before—as adequate preparation for his position in social work. He confessed openly that nothing he had learned in school had actually been of help in this job and that he had forgotten much of what he had studied so long ago anyway.

He was correct in one respect: An opposing attorney might have chosen to challenge his educational credentials. What he did not understand, however, is that every expert witness may be seriously challenged about credentials. Principles for answering such challenges do exist, and they consist of the following three guidelines:

1. Understand that for each of us, no matter how well qualified in education or training or experience, there are numerous more-or-less relevant things that we are not as professionals:

that is, things that we have not studied, that we are not certified to do, and about which we are not competent. A good attorney during cross-examination may choose to bring such gaps to the surface.

2. Within ourselves, we need to accept that we do not have universal wisdom or comprehensive education. That acceptance should be acknowledged on the witness stand in a matter-of-fact manner.

3. It is defensiveness and discomfort about credentials that make us less credible, not the credentials themselves. The witnesses who are comfortable and understanding about discussing their limitations are the ones for whom the limitations do not seem, well, limiting.

These principles may be tried in response to the following attorney questions:

Q: "Surely, Mr. Jones, you would not tell this court that your major in history at college, in any way, shape, or form, prepared you for the interviewing and professional skills needed to be a good social worker?"

The simplest and easiest reply is a nondefensive, "Of course not." The witness who awkwardly attempts to connect the study of history to the study of human problems would be seen as straining. The witness who chose at this point to discuss the agency training and other, more recent acquisition of expertise might also do well. However, such explanations can be made only when the launch window is open for them. Otherwise, defensiveness and low credibility come across much more than does expertise.

The more typical questions are not about BA education for positions normally staffed at higher educational levels but about credentials not achieved. Suppose that the cross-examining attorney knows from omissions in the direct examination and from the witness's résumé that a doctorate in psychology or medicine is not accompanied by being certified by the witness's professional certifying board. The attorney might then ask these questions:

Q: "Doctor, what does it mean to be board-certified?"

Q: "Board-certification, then, represents *assurance* of advanced competence and excellence?"

Q: "And, Doctor, are *you* board-certified?"

Many variations on this credentialing challenge exist. To the witness who has not published, the attorney may ask:

Q: "Exactly how many articles have you written for professional or scientific journals?"

Q: "Not even one, in any journal, anywhere?"

To psychologists and social workers, attorneys sometimes ask,

Q: "You are not a medical doctor, is that correct?"

Q: "Isn't it true you are not allowed to practice medicine in this state, or in any other state in this country?"

Q: "Isn't it true that some mental disorders actually have their origin in the brain?"

Q: "And isn't it correct that you are neither qualified nor allowed to medicate the brain or operate on the brain?"

For psychiatrists and physicians, a parallel series of questions is sometimes posed that forces them to admit how untrained they are in psychology.

Q: "Have you had graduate-level courses in memory and perception? In intelligence testing? In the psychology of learning?"

Attorneys succeed in these questions if the witness overexplains and is too self-protective. Attorneys also succeed if the witness is made to sound wounded. Thus, the credible witness answers "that is correct" with the same demeanor and feeling tone that would be presented to an inquiry about a current address or title. Given the opportunity, the witness might choose to explain in a narrative form, such as,

"I have not yet exercised my option to apply for board certification."

"While some psychologists spend their careers writing and publishing, my emphasis has been on helping and evaluating people."

"My specialty is psychology, not psychiatry, and it is psychology that I am licensed to practice."

"I would no more perform brain surgery than a brain surgeon

would administer psychological tests. We are in different professions."

"Although I have not had formal courses in memory and perception, every psychiatrist is trained to understand the fundamental role these individual factors have in people's lives and adjustments."

Witnesses do not have to make these explanatory statements. If qualifications they do not have are accurately identified, it is satisfactory to agree straightforwardly. Judges and jurors are not taken in by such challenges unless the witnesses themselves are affected. Fuller explanations should be considered desirable but by no means necessary when credentials are aggressively challenged.

THE MAXIM: *Comfortably agree with accurate challenges to your credentials. Offer narrative explanations only when they are nondefensive and unforced.*

❧ 19 ❧

Culturally Different Clients

YOU ARE TESTIFYING ABOUT AN EVALUATION OF A client who is a relatively new arrival from a culture quite different from yours. Whatever the reason for the evaluation and your conclusions, you find yourself challenged in cross-examination about your ability to understand the meaning of psychopathological issues within that culture. This challenge may have sound foundations. Dohrenwend and Dohrenwend (1974), in a review of epidemiological studies of psychopathology, found few worldwide consistencies. Indeed, even the nature of a particular culture to be studied is often unclear, and psychological differences may be found on the basis of nationality, tribal identity, language, and ethnic group (Draguns, 1982).

For the mental health clinician, perhaps the essential question is whether culture-free definitions of abnormal behaviors are present. Competence, autonomy, perception of reality, self-actualization, resistance to stress, and balance of psychic forces have been described by some authorities as truly cross-cultural; however, the same criteria have been severely criticized as themselves being culture-bound and vague (Sarbin & Juhasz, 1982). The clinician's task before testifying is to have a degree of cultural relativism, so that other cultural patterns are not translated routinely into your cultural norms and understandings.

Suppose you have testified that a Native American Cherokee father would be a poor parent if he were granted custody of his child, among other reasons because he is totally uninvolved in parental duties such as discipline. A question from the attorney for the father might be,

"Are you aware that in many Cherokee communities, relatives other than the parents assume primary responsibility for discipline and guidance?" (No.)

"Would information of that sort have been useful in conducting your evaluation for custody?"

The no response reflects the general lack of knowledge about Native American culture. A good reply to the second question would acknowledge the potential use of such information while at the same time addressing the actual findings of *this* child's needs.

Another example can relate to immigrants from India. Assume a personal injury suit in which, among other claims, an Indian man has been distressed by his increased masturbation after the accident, and your expert testimony for the defense has minimized this claim of emotional disability. A wise plaintiff's attorney might ask:

"Are you familiar with the Indian expression 'one drop of semen is worth forty drops of blood?' "

"Based on your knowledge of Indian culture, please explain in your own words what this concept might mean for Mr. Krishna."

"Answer the same question for anyone else raised in the semen-loss belief system of India."

The correct answer is that for Indian Hindus, loss of semen is equated to loss of life and vital energies, and masturbation is taken more seriously and traumatically than in the United States. The issue might then be put in context by a knowledgeable witness with an elaboration such as this one: "Although Mr. Krishna explained to me the seriousness of his concern about masturbation, in the overall picture of his emotional adjustment, I found only the modest disruptions I've already noted."

If you have never heard of the semen-loss concept, an honest admission is in order, possibly accompanied by a clear restatement of the actual foundations and data from which your inferences were drawn.

Similar scenarios could be constructed for every culture. With Japanese clients who never looked the examiner in the eye, this behavior has sometimes been used to suggest psychopathology. During cross-examination, a lawyer might correctly tap into the regular avoidance of eye contact as a sign of deference and respect in subordinate–superior interactions in Japan. Thus, culture-free assumptions about mental health assessments can be quite weak. The prepared clinician-witnesses will have read about the culture from which their clients come, will have talked about the culture with experts if possible and surely with the client, and will be educated about the cultural and subcultural contexts of all their clients.

THE MAXIM: *Culture does affect the*
assessment of psychopathology.
Witnesses should be culture educated
while still clearly identifying and affirming the
conventional foundations of their testimony.

❦ 20 ❦

The Direct Examination

THE MEDICATION WAS DULLING THE PAIN FROM MY lower back as I lay still in bed, knees elevated to keep my spine straight, when the telephone rang and an attorney asked me to testify in court in forty-five minutes. I protested that I had only committed myself to testify the next week, as the attorney had earlier estimated. The trial was moving fast, I was told. Could I please be there? My testimony was important.

I declined at first. My back hurt. My thinking was blurry. My consciousness was impaired by the medication. The attorney appealed to my vulnerability, telling me how much I was needed. I asked if he would sign an informed consent statement affirming that he knew what he was getting if I testified in this handicapped state. He knew.

Within the hour I walked up to the witness stand with the ginger, guarded movements of someone carrying stacks of expensive glassware. With difficulty I was able to attend and respond to the qualifying questions and the major areas of testimony we had discussed. The attorney then asked a question we had never discussed:

"Doctor, isn't nervousness while being interviewed a sign that a person may be lying?"

I declined to answer directly. I explained that it might or might not be true. He tried again, rephrasing the question. I spoke about nervousness as potentially being a sign of many things. He persisted. I strained hard to determine whether it was my impaired state that was the problem while explaining how nervousness cannot always be assessed in terms of causes. Finally, he asked if it was *possible* that lying could cause nervousness in the key witness.

"Sure," I replied.

"Thank you, doctor," he chirped, and he concluded the direct examination triumphantly.

Except for my physical problem (which did not absolve me of responsibility to testify well), this experience is not unusual. Attorneys may ask direct-examination questions that surprise the expert. I have seen attorneys conduct direct examination as if they were cross-examinations, grilling the witness in an attacking, critical manner. Some preventive steps may avoid such unpleasant surprises.

First, meet with the attorneys before the trial and go over the questions to be asked. If the witness knows the questions and has thought about the answers in advance, then there will be fewer surprises. Indeed, a secure feeling may come from knowing the demands that will initiate one's testimony.

Second, feel free to reshape and rephrase the questions, to tap what is known and what can be said. Attorneys do not always know the best ways to phrase questions, and most attorneys welcome this help.

Third, as noted earlier, give the attorneys a list of qualifying questions about employment, education, experience, skills, publications, honors, and so on. Attorneys have differing levels of mastery of this part of the examination, and a prepared list of the qualifying questions can be useful to them.

Fourth, in areas of testimony about which you have uncertainties, discuss with the attorneys how to include those uncertainties in the direct examination. Two-sided arguments are more persuasive than one-sided arguments in such instances.

Fifth, do not try to second-guess an unclear question. You may answer, "I do not understand the thrust of your question. Could you ask it in a different way?"

Finally, when there have been insufficient opportunities to meet with the attorney, do not try to overly interpret on the stand what the attorney is trying to do. Simply answer the questions with integrity and without second-guessing. That tactic maintains the witness's impartiality and credibility.

THE MAXIM: *Meet with the attorney prior to the direct examination and be involved in preparing the questions.*

❧ 21 ❧

Disaster Relief

IN THE TRIAL EXPERIENCE OF ALL EXPERTS, THERE comes a time when they say something outright wrong or foolish. These blunders may arise because opposing attorneys develop a line of questioning that leads to foolishness. They may arise because the experts are nervous on the witness stand and, as a consequence, they think slowly and poorly. The blunders may even arise from that least acceptable of all possibilities—defensive ignorance—in which the experts seek to conceal their lack of knowledge by putting forth replies that mimic accurate knowledge.

Whatever the cause, these disastrous blunders haunt experts. I often begin my expert witness workshops by asking the participants to describe their worst experiences in court and in turn I relate mine. Participants report these disasters with vivid recall, describing how they felt trapped, humiliated, as if a noose were tightening around their necks. Elsewhere in this book I discuss preventive skills. However, the present concern is with disaster relief, what to do after the earthquake has split your professional esteem into apparently unrecoverable shards.

In the instances in which the attorney has changed topic,

witnesses need to let go of their distress. The typical pattern is a continued mental dwelling on that catastrophic moment, so that witnesses feel bad, listen poorly, and carry along the disaster in their minds. This perseverance is dysfunctional. Instead of managing the immediate questions, the witnesses desperately want to make things right. Occasionally, witnesses will try to go back to the prior topic. Sometimes volunteering that you just realized you answered a previous question incorrectly, and asking if the judge (or the attorney) would like you to correct it, will lead to the chance to restate an answer. At other times that effort is met by a brusque dismissal. The experts do not have the procedural right to direct the content of the cross-examination. In the latter case, the only solution is to clear the mind, let go of the residual self-blame, and not worry. Although this letting go is not easily achieved, an intense focus on the current questions does help.

Sometimes witnesses realize they have blundered while the same line of questions is in progress. The cross-examining attorney builds on the foolish response by expanding the scope of the inquiry and extending the damage from the witness's catastrophically bad answer. This powerful process happened to me when an attorney had just maneuvered me to admit that I had not read an expensive, detailed study on an institution I had inspected. He had asked why I had not read this most thorough, most costly, most detailed study. Without thinking ahead, I answered that I would have read it if I knew he was going to ask me all of these questions about it. The attorney should have settled for that victory. Instead, he became greedy and asked more questions about my failure to know the results of the study. I finally recovered sufficiently to comment that the expensive study was somebody else's opinion and that what was important in this evaluation was *my own* assessment.

When the attorney is actively expanding on the disastrous answer, witnesses do have the opportunity to correct themselves. I suggest a simple and straightforward correction, something like this:

"A few minutes ago, I suggested that I knew about genetic foundations of human behavior. That was in error. If I gave the impression for even a second that I was an expert on genetics, I need to take that back right now. Actually, my area of expertise is psychotherapeutic practice and not at all genetics related to disease patterns."

That kind of correction shuts off the attorney's questions. Once witnesses have corrected themselves, they no longer are subjected to a long, painful line of questions that enlarge the blunder. Instead, they may have successfully recanted and regained their credibility.

THE MAXIM: *After a disaster during testimony, correct the error as soon as you can. If you cannot, let it go.*

❧ 22 ❧

DSM Cautions

ONE OF THE FACTS OF LIFE IN DIAGNOSIS of psychological disorders is that diagnosticians use and depend on the American Psychiatric Association's *Diagnostic and Statistical Manual of Mental Disorders (DSM)*. In its various revisions, the *DSM* has always included a statement in the introduction or set off by itself cautioning the user about legal applications of these diagnoses. Even the most thorough clinicians tend to skim through these introductory notes in order to get to the core, the actual descriptions of disorders and their diagnostic criteria. Now and then a careful attorney will ask cross-examination questions about this introductory caution. The questions go like this:

"Have you read the *Diagnostic and Statistical Manual of Mental Disorders* by the American Psychiatric Association?" (Yes.)

"Do you depend heavily on these diagnostic categories and criteria in reaching your conclusions?" (Yes.)

"Do you accept the writers and framers of this manual as experts in these matters?" (Yes.)

"Are you familiar with the warning at the beginning of this

manual on page xxix against applying these diagnostic categories to legal issues or judgments?" (No.)

"Why have you not read and heeded these warnings of the foremost authorities in your field against using the *DSM* diagnoses in legal issues?"

At this point, witnesses sometimes feel cornered. Before suggestions are made as to possible responses, let us look at the statement of caution as written in the *DSM-III-R.* Future editions of the *DSM* are likely to have similar statements.

> It is to be understood that inclusion here, for clinical and research purposes, of a diagnostic category such as Pathological Gambling or Pedophilia does not imply that the condition meets legal or other nonmedical criteria for what constitutes mental disease, mental disorder, or mental disability. The clinical and scientific considerations involved in categorizations of these conditions as mental disorders may not be wholly relevant to legal judgments, for example, that take into account such issues as individual responsibility, disability determination, and competency. (American Psychiatric Association, 1987, p. xxix)

This cautionary statement is ambiguous. When the phrase "such as Pathological Gambling or Pedophilia" is used, the reader is unclear how broad the reach of such diagnoses may be. In the same sense, the phrase "may not be wholly relevant" does not mean the same as irrelevant. Rather, the phrase describes an extensive range from almost wholly relevant to legal judgments down to partially relevant and all the way to irrelevant. The term *may be* is equally mushy. The more important part of the caution is the warning against wholesale application of diagnostic concepts to legal conclusions, a principle with which most clinicians would agree. Thus, some proper responses to the last of the sample cross-examination questions could be,

"Every one of us in this field seeks to fully heed this warning.

It would be inappropriate and irresponsible for me or anyone to present psychological diagnoses as legal judgments."

or

"The role of mental health professionals is to make mental health judgments, which I do, and not legal conclusions."

or

"It's unnecessary to read and memorize such a basic principle that we are taught repeatedly, from our first courses onward. And I unequivocally endorse and practice using caution in applying diagnoses to legal questions, in every issue, from commitment of the mentally disordered to assessment of criminal responsibility."

Mental health experts should remember that they are testifying as health professionals and only as health professionals. That awareness helps them brush off this challenge to their proper role in participation in legal processes. Of course, this particular cross-examination effort is attempted only when the attorney either has no mental health expert of his or her own or, if the *DSM* questioning succeeds, is willing to sacrifice the credibility of experts on both sides.

THE MAXIM: *Do not be befuddled if you do not know specific* DSM *cautions. Do affirm the underlying principles of such cautions in which you believe.*

Elder Abuse and Neglect

THE NEGLECT AND ABUSE OF ELDERLY PEOPLE IS a long-hidden problem that has been moving into public awareness. Acts of neglect
and abuse are rarely deliberate, malicious choices. Rather, they are
part of personal ineptness by the elderly person and the younger
caretaker alike. Sometimes an incontinent older man or woman
profoundly frustrates an adult child who cleans and serves the elderly parent. An unemployed and alcoholic son in his midfifties may
not bring enough food to his mother. Resentment, anger, and verbal
abuse accumulate, often with no easy solution (McDowell, 1989).

Professionals become involved because someone is hurt or
unable to manage finances. Some cases lead to an adult protective
services office acting to initiate guardianship, a placement, or, occasionally, criminal charges because of physical force resulting in
injuries. Many professionals are uncomfortable in such work because
they see all participants as victims. The murky ambiguity of so many
of these situations makes it worse for many professionals. Yet involved they get, and sometimes that means testifying in court.

To be a persuasive, effective expert witness on elder abuse

and neglect calls for specific knowledge. Assuming that there will be a full transfer of learning from your own discipline to the area of elder abuse is not justified. My observations are that the theoretical and practical aspects of elder abuse must be understood in their own right and challenges to knowledge in the courtroom should be anticipated (Brodsky, 1989a).

Here are four sample questions that an alert attorney might pose during a cross-examination:

"Isn't it true that some elderly people become very susceptible to bruising from firm pressure [to keep them from falling]?"

"Now, you weren't actually there at the time of these alleged assaults, were you?"

"Isn't it true that competency is not a single ability but the sum of abilities to complete hundreds of daily tasks?"

"Are you familiar with the book on competence assessment by Dr. Thomas Grisso?" (Brodsky, 1989a, pp. 12–14)

The first question might be handled by staying only with the actual observation of the bruises rather than presenting oneself as an expert on the physiology of bruises. The second question calls for a simple, nondefensive acknowledgment.

The third and fourth questions are intended to make the testifying professional feel inadequate. The responsive (and responsible) answer affirms what one does and does not know. If the attorney correctly states your limits on understanding of competence, let it be. It is okay to simply say yes to the third question and no to the fourth question. However, the better alternatives are to be able to discuss the concept of competence and to be an informed consumer of Grisso's (1986) excellent book.

Testifying about elder abuse is talking about a sensitive area. The events are often tragic. Although acting professional is vital, being empathic and human are equally important. Do not let the court setting depersonalize you. Instead, allow concern to be seen as much as professionalism. The elder abuse and neglect subject calls for such openness.

THE MAXIM: *Testimony about elder abuse calls for a mixture of specific expertise and visible empathy.*

❧ 24 ❧

Employment Discrimination

THE FORMAL STATEMENT OF THE LAW AGAINST DISCRIMINATION in employment is straightforward enough. If an employer has good reason to believe that selection for employment or promotion excludes individuals by race, sex, or ethnic group, the employer needs to take affirmative action to correct the exclusion. The decisions about exactly what procedures make up exclusionary policies or what action constitutes adequate affirmative actions are not always so straightforward. Robinson (1980) has pointed out some of these difficulties. Is it acceptable, Robinson asked, for Chinese restaurants to exclude for employment everyone other than Chinese applicants? Is it acceptable, taking this reasoning one step further, for only Italians to be employed in a Chinese restaurant? This example is not hypothetical. One Chinese restaurant in London did hire only Italian waiters. The expert witnesses who testify about employment discrimination deal with more empirical, but no less intriguing, issues.

When individuals or groups feel that they have been unfairly denied employment on the bases of race, sex, or ethnic group, they file claims with the Equal Employment Opportunity Commission (EEOC). Expert witnesses in the cases address the distribution of the allegedly discriminated persons in hired and nonhired groups, and testify about the selection practices.

Kurtz and McClung (1974) have discussed the examination of expert witnesses in EEOC cases, critiquing the typical questions asked by attorneys and the responses of witnesses. In the presentation of the plaintiff's case (i.e., the complaining parties), the attorney for the defense often asks the opposing witness during the cross-examination if he or she is familiar with the testing guidelines of the EEOC (1990) and the American Psychological Association (APA, 1985). After the witness has answered yes, the cross-examining attorney can usually find and describe a discrepancy between the EEOC or APA standards and the witness's testimony. Finding a discrepancy is not difficult because so few of these rigorous guidelines are ever fully implemented in practice. The next question that follows is, "Is it not fair to say, then, that your opinions concerning test validation are not necessarily in full accord with these documents?" (Kurtz & McClung, 1974, p. 9).

That question is designed to make the witness feel isolated from accepted standards and, or course, guilty about that isolation. How to answer that kind of question? Here are two possibilities:

"No." This one-word answer usually forces the attorney to ask additional questions, gives the witness a chance to explain, and shifts power to the witness.

"Full accord. Perhaps not. I know of few professionals who are. I am, however, in general accord with these documents" (Kurtz & McClung, 1974, p. 9). This second response demonstrated a careful listening to the question. The key words in the question were "full accord," and the witness neatly put this concept in practical context.

Other issues also emerge in cross-examination of plaintiffs' witnesses. One essential question asked is, "Isn't it true that in every administrative, testing, scoring, and employment step that minority applications were treated objectively the same as other applicants? That is, weren't the steps such that a blind person working only with numbers would come up with the same results?"

In reply, the witness might discuss the first part of the question first. Instead of answering yes, the witness could point out that the steps or measures are not accepted by him or her and that a substantial difference exists between *truly* objective and *seemingly* objective measures. Once this distinction has been made, the witness may appropriately qualify the answer.

When witnesses for the defense are being cross-examined, the questions are often directed toward the nature and causes of de facto discrimination. These challenges to the defendant's hiring practices are typically met by clear statements that

- General social inequality limits the pool of qualified applicants. For a position that requires a college education or graduate degree, fewer minorities have such credentials, and it is the pool of college-educated minorities, not the population pool, that needs to be the base of comparison.
- Out of fairness to *all* applicants, standardized and objective screening measures are used.
- Good employment-screening measures are always criterion related; it is who can do the job who gets hired.[1]

In some complex cases, reasonable experts can differ on the fairness of employment practices. In this discussion I have not sought to address such issues. The question addressed here has been how witnesses can best defend their own responsible knowledge during cross-examinations.

---

[1] Tom Grisso has pointed out to me that these three points have been effective arguments in the hands of psychologists working for the gold mining industry in South Africa. In that industry, the testing and selection practices make it very difficult for Black workers to be promoted to shift foreman positions.

THE MAXIM: *In equal opportunity cases, plaintiff witnesses need to focus on social context and defense witnesses on objective comparisons.*

❧ 25 ❧

Examiner Effects

THE TERM *EXAMINER EFFECTS* HAS BEEN USED TO describe the entire range of nonobvious influences a psychological examiner has on a client. Thus, at the simplest demographic level, male examiners may produce different client behaviors than female examiners, White examiners may elicit different behaviors than examiners of other racial backgrounds, and young examiners may have different stimulus values than older examiners. Examiner effects extend potentially to the effects of one's working psychological theory, to attitudes, to religious, political, and socioeconomic status groups to which examiners and clients belong, and to the warmth and empathy of the examiner. The latter variable is especially influential. Clients disclose more to examiners who are seen as being more understanding, caring, and warm. Indeed, Jourard (1971) proposed that the scientific role of psychological researchers as objective, detached, and uninvolved so strongly influences subject behaviors that all psychological research with human beings needs to redone with warm, empathic examiners in order to get balanced, meaningful results.

Mental health professionals find it difficult to really know their personal examiner effects because, like all of us, their stimulus values are with them all of the time. The examiners attribute variance from normal or expected behaviors to clients without realizing how much clients may vary from situation to situation and examiner to examiner. Put another way, mental health professionals see client behaviors that, to a fair degree, may be states and interpret them as traits.

When challenged on the witness stand about examiner effects, expert witnesses should reply on the basis of the components of training, supervision, consultation, structured and objective procedures, and standardized clinical interviews. The reason supervisors and consultants listen to and watch tapes, observe through closed-circuit television or mirrors, and give feedback to the clinician is to educate about and reduce examiner effects. In the same sense, witnesses should be prepared to talk about standardized interviews and objective assessments as ways in which examiner variability is controlled. Given these principles, the reader may wish to see how well she or he would do in responding to a tough questioning about these issues. Consider a cross-examination sequence about examiner effects drawn from the Ziskin (1981) book, *Coping With Psychiatric and Psychological Testimony* (3rd ed.). This exchange is taken exactly from the Ziskin book, except that the questions and answers are numbered.

>   *Q1:* Are you familiar with the term examiner effects?
>
>   *A1:* Yes (If no, the cross-examiner will have to explain this).
>
>   *Q2:* What does that term mean in relation to the diagnostic process?
>
>   *A2:* It has to do with the fact that characteristics of the examiner may have an influence on the diagnostic process.
>
>   *Q3:* Would examiner effects include such things as the examiner's theoretical orientation, and his personality, and his social and political values and attitudes?
>
>   *A3:* Yes.

Q4: Do these examiner effects have some influence on the data that is [sic] obtained?

A4: Yes.

Q5: Do they also have some influence on the data the examiner will pay attention to or record?

A5: Yes.

Q6: And do they also have an influence on the way he interprets the data of the clinical examination?

A6: Yes.

Q7: So then, some examiners with one theoretical orientation might get different data and record different data and interpret the data differently than an examiner of a different theoretical orientation, is that correct?

A7: Yes.

Q8: And also, examiners with different personalities might get some different kinds of information from the people they examine, isn't that correct?

A8: Yes, that is correct.

Q9: That's because people respond differently to different types of people, isn't that so?

A9: That is so.

Q10: So the material produced in the interview results, to some extent, from the conditions of the examination and the type of examiner conducting the examination, isn't that correct?

A10: No. I wouldn't say that's correct because the data is [sic] still coming from the person being examined.

Q11: Yes, but if he were being examined under different circumstances, by a psychiatrist with a different theoretical orientation, and a different personality, different needs, values, and biases, he might produce different data, isn't that correct?

A11: Yes, that is correct.

Q12: And it is the data from the examination that determines what the diagnosis is going to be, isn't that correct?

> *A12:* Yes, that's correct. (Ziskin, 1981, Vol. 2, p. 86)

A critique of this witness might begin by noting that no active explanations appeared until *A10*, in which a partial answer is offered. This answer missed the key part of *Q10*, which was the phrase "to some extent." Even if a witness chose to wait until that point to explain, the explanation might well focus on how this process is influential to a tiny extent, and why.

Opportunities appear much earlier to take control. In *A2*, the witness might have said, "It has to do with the possibility, particularly for examiners using idiosyncratic clinical procedures, that the characteristics of the examiner may influence the diagnostic process."

If the witness chose to wait until *A7* or *A8* to explain, the answer might well be "No, quite to the contrary. The nature of the clinical method and the mental status examination in mental health interviewing is to use standard questions asked in a neutral manner and tone of voice, the answers to which are compared with a substantial base of normative client replies." For the questions with which everyone would agree, the witness might respond enthusiastically and with a comment. Thus, in reply to *Q9*, the witness might have said:

"Actually, they respond similarly to various examiners in many basic and important ways, but slightly different in other ways. A chameleon still looks like a chameleon, no matter what color it changes to.[1] But that's not a psychiatric principle, but rather just part of good, common sense that everyone knows."

If the cross-examiner pursues this further, the witness should

---

[1] Originally, I treated this as a situation for a push–pull answer, suggesting that the witness say, "Oh, they most certainly do respond differently to different types of people." The reply now presented here was a suggestion from Tom Grisso, which I have used in its entirety. It works much better.

go back to the principles of training, supervision, and standardized procedures. These principles do, in fact, set aside professionals from laypeople in abilities to know about the impact on others' behaviors.

The Maxim: *Cross-examinations about examiner effects call for the witness to explain how training and standardized procedures diminish such effects.*

❧ 26 ❧

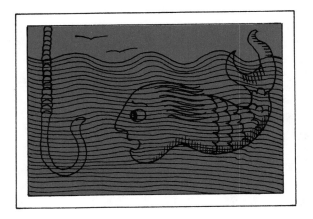

Fishing Expeditions

ONE STYLE OF ATTORNEY QUESTIONS IN DEPOSITIONS AND cross-examinations is the "fishing expedition." In this pattern, the attorney casts questions out to a wide range of possible matters, scanning for deficiencies in content or for signs that the expert witness is uncomfortable. Once the vulnerable area is located, the attorney directs much effort to setting the hook, that is, to expose ignorance and insecurity.

The fishing analogy may be extended to witnesses' responses. The courtroom-knowledgeable witness recognizes the fishing expedition and simply does not take the bait. With no nibbles, the attorney either casts again or gives up, trying always to close on a note of apparent success.

The best questions of this sort begin with fundamentals. I hear warning bells chiming loudly in my head when an opposing attorney asks me basic questions such as these, taken from a case in which an incidental part of the findings is that the defendant is schizophrenic:

"What is schizophrenia?"

"Are there different theories about the nature of schizophrenia?"

"How has the definition of schizophrenia changed with the various revisions of diagnostic codes over the years?"

"Why is it there is so much scientific dispute about the existence of different forms of schizophrenia?"

"Why is it possible for one well-trained clinician to conclude that a person is schizophrenic and for another well-trained clinician to conclude that the same person is not schizophrenic?"

"Do you subscribe to and conscientiously read any of the journals devoted fully to research in schizophrenia?"

"What courses have you taken that have been devoted fully to the study of schizophrenia?"

None of these questions require that the attorney know the answers. In fact, the attorneys typically do not. Instead, the questions are part of an intelligent way to pose questions to probe for ignorance or discomfort. If the witness is indeed an expert on schizophrenia per se, then these questions may be answered precisely and authoritatively. The attorney, however, is gambling that the witness is not an expert on schizophrenia.

The first question on "what is schizophrenia" should be met with a simple, straightforward definition. The subsequent questions require a clear delineation of present roles and knowledge. Some suggested answers include components of role delineation, referral, and restatement of findings:

"My position is as a clinical practitioner, not as a researcher [role delineation]. If the court needs expertise in history and research in schizophrenia, you would need to bring in somebody else [referral]. However, I am happy to share with the court exactly how Mr. Smith's disorder and suicidal thoughts make it really risky to leave him on his own in the community [restatement of findings]."

The fishing expedition just illustrated catches the expert with hubris, that is, with arrogance and lack of humility. By the way, such arrogance is not necessarily a long-standing trait and can be brought out just by being on the witness stand and having the feeling that one ought to know just about everything about everything. Once witnesses do start to testify about content about which they have fragmentary knowledge, watch out! The skilled attorney will lead such witnesses along the fishing expedition and will land them hard once they have bitten. The wise witness will stay carefully within the bounds of what he or she does and knows.

THE MAXIM: *When the attorney fishes for ignorance and insecurities, keep your knowledge limits clearly in mind.*

❖ 27 ❖

Fraternization During the Trial

MOST OF WITNESSES' ATTENTION IS DIRECTED TOWARD THEIR conduct on the witness stand. However, considerable interaction with others may take place during recesses, breaks, preceding and following testimony, and at other times and places. Conversations can arise in the witness room, in corridors outside of the courtroom, and sometimes in the courtroom itself. Some witnesses find themselves talking with other witnesses, opposing counsel, reporters, jurors, clients, clients' relatives, police officers, or students. I advise reticence and caution.

Consider the situation in which opposing attorneys or their assistants greet you in an affable and engaging manner and then move the subject to issues in your forthcoming testimony or issues being tried. Here is a scenario from a book about malpractice that illustrates what can develop:

> After the amenities, conversation may turn to what has just happened on the witness stand, an item of evidence, or a medical point in the case. A naive defendant may inadvertently educate the attorney for the plaintiff or a codefendant who is

87

> an opponent in regard to some medical aspect of the case or other fact that he was not aware of. Such a physician may reveal the name of a witness or information about a witness that allows his opponent to prepare more thoroughly for cross-examination. (Alton, 1977, p. 214)

Some attorneys approach witnesses in the corridors or during breaks with such an easy, enthusiastic style that the witnesses want to talk at length to these charming folks. Don't! I speak readily about the weather, I suppose, but I monitor my words with care and say nothing about any aspect of the case. That closed-mouth attitude extends to not talking about other witnesses, about other trials in which I have testified, or how long I have been involved in the present case. As politely as possible, I explain that we need to hold off just now on talking business. They understand.

Sometimes other witnesses waiting to testify begin conversations about their role or the trial. Occasionally, jurors are waiting in line at the water fountain, soft drink machines, or snack bars and say hello and initiate conversations. If you have assessed a criminal defendant or civil action plaintiff, the client may feel a continuing rapport and seek to add more information or to chat personally. The same cautions apply. Speak minimally and only in amenities. Conversations with witnesses or jurors can contaminate the trial, and conversations with clients in the court setting can appear to compromise the objectivity of the expert role.

In one case in which I was helping strike a jury, I was observing the jury veniremen reporting for duty and being briefed by the judge. A woman in the jury pool sat next to me and repeatedly attempted to converse. I kept putting my finger to my lips and pointing to the front of the courtroom. Because she persisted, I moved, and she followed, only this time passing me notes to read. My silence and nonresponsiveness eventually did deter her, but it was a lesson in this art of what I might call "zen nonfraternization": being there but not having an active presence.

THE MAXIM: *Neither fraternize nor discuss any element of the case with opposing counsel, other witnesses, clients, or jurors.*

❧ 28 ❧

Freud as an Expert Witness

HOW WOULD FREUD HAVE BEEN AS AN EXPERT witness? In his long career, Freud actually did serve once as an expert witness (Eissler, 1986). During World War I, thousands of Austrian soldiers who were either "war neurotics" or malingerers had been treated with electrical currents, emetics, substances that produced nausea, and isolation at the psychiatric clinic of Dr. Julius Wagner-Jauregg. Dr. Wagner was a prominent Viennese psychiatrist who, in 1928, was given the Nobel prize for his development of malaria treatment for general paresis in mental patients.

In December 1918, the provisional National Assembly of an Austria demoralized and devastated by the war established a commission to investigate, among other issues, psychiatric treatment of soldiers as patients. Wagner was accused of the cruelty and torture of Walter Kauders, who had been wounded in battle by an exploding shell. Freud wrote a report for the commission and on October 14, 1920, Freud presented testimony and was questioned by the chairman of the commission and by other participants. My comments about Freud's responses as an expert witness are presented in brackets after each statement. Freud had begun with an assessment of the accusations against Wagner that concluded that disagreements between physicians and patients come about when patients feel they are not understood (Eissler, 1986, pp. 69–70).

"Chairman: Do you believe that such disagreements can be avoided?"

"Professor Freud: If these patients had been psychoanalytically examined as well, such accusations would never have been made." [Freud not only answers the question with an implicit yes, he goes well beyond the scope of the question to identify psychoanalytic approaches as the solution.]

"Witness Kauders: May I ask you, Professor: Do you, or do you not, consider it a questionable thing for a mentally normal person to be locked in a cell under the encroachment of madmen for seventy-seven days, as I was?"

"Professor Freud: I consider isolation like this to be very unpleasant but completely without risk."

[Considerable reasons at that time and at the present time exist to disagree with the substance of Freud's response. However, the answer itself is masterful. It identifies the commonsense awareness of the discomfort of long isolation, and yet, in a modified admit–deny format, presents a clear and compelling conclusion.]

A brief discussion followed of whether electrical treatment is painful or not, in which Freud comments, "There are people who find that very unpleasant." Then, the previous topic is again addressed.

"Engineer Kunzel: Please allow me one more question. From the scientific point of view, do you think it is justified to keep a patient in solitary confinement for seventy-seven days, even assuming that he is malingering? You have made a statement on the principle of solitary confinement, but just seventy-seven days are curative?"

"Professor Freud: Are you referring to the evenness or the unevenness of the number?"

[Freud's answer here is in part in response to a pun not easily translatable. The German word for "just" can also mean "even."

However, Freud's choice of this response indicates a brief putting off of a reply, perhaps while he considered the question. His reply also has a slight quality of either petulance or what Eissler feels is irritability. In any case, Freud did not respond directly to the question.]

"Engineer Kunzel: I mean the length of time."

"Professor Freud: This whole therapy is not my own. I would not have done all these things. . . . I think not. Naturally I am not on the whole in favor of this kind of treatment in cases of malingering. The whole thing is contradictory. . . ." (Eissler, 1986, pp. 70–72.)

[Now Freud comes to the point. His statements were unequivocal. He identified his own work as his frame of reference and rejected the Wagner methods. Later in this same statement he offered justification for these conclusions. Here he was an outstanding witness.]

Two days later, when the commission hearings resumed, other prominent psychiatrists attacked Freud's testimony. They indicated that psychoanalysis could not work with poor people, that its length was impractical for wide applications, and that Freud had never seen war neuroses and knew nothing about them.

One psychiatrist testified that he had tried psychoanalysis before the war and had no success whatsoever. Another psychiatrist with psychoanalytic training testified that "we can say with psychoanalysis we cannot achieve in two years what faradization [electrical current treatment] can do in two hours or isolation in a few weeks" (Eissler, 1986, p. 94). The eventual outcome was that Dr. Wagner was completely exonerated.

Overall, Freud was a good expert witness, at least in responding to the specific questions I have reviewed. He was confident, assertive, and in control. Today's expert witnesses should be pleased to do as well.

THE MAXIM: *When testifying about something in which you believe, testify in a manner that shows that you believe in it.*

❧ 29 ❧

The Historic Hysteric Gambit

AT TIMES OF DESPERATION AND INABILITY TO SCRATCH the solid foundation of an expert's testimony, attorneys sometimes resort to attacking the whole discipline or profession of the witness. This technique is used when the immediate cross-examination battle has been lost and when the attorneys do not have witnesses of their own from the same profession. A particularly well-thought-out and charming version of this technique has been described by James McConnell (1969), of worm-running and undergraduate psychology text fame, as the "historic hysteric" gambit. This gambit calls for the attorneys to expose the absurdities in the history of the profession in order to dent the shining professional armor of the witness.

Almost any example of foolish things once accepted by the professional field can be used in the historic hysteric gambit. Attorneys examining physicians may, for example, ask about the treatment of President James Garfield after he was shot on July 3, 1881. Garfield apparently died from the infections caused by physicians repeatedly probing the bullet in the open wound with their unwashed fingers. McConnell (1969) has suggested that any professional field may be attacked by drawing on examples of the smug and hostile receptions the medical communities made to the discoveries of Ignaz Semmelweiss, Louis Pasteur, and Alexander Fleming. A typical line of questioning might go like this:

"Doctor, does the name Ignaz Semmelweiss ring a bell?" [I advise witnesses to be selective in responding by saying, "No, but the name Pavlov does ring a bell."]

Whether the witness agrees or not, the attorney goes on:

"Isn't Semmelweiss the Viennese physician of the 1860s who proposed that doctors should wash the blood and pus from autopsies off their hands before delivering babies?"

"Would it surprise you to know that the entire Viennese medical community ridiculed Semmelweiss, insulted him, and forced him to leave his job and Vienna?"

"And, doctor, didn't all of those physicians of Vienna think they were right, just as you physicians [or psychologists or social workers] all think you are right in what you do and conclude today?"

A parallel line of questions can been organized about Sir Alexander Fleming, the Nobel Prize winner and discoverer of penicillin (McConnell, 1969, p. 68). These questions begin by asking if the witness is familiar with Fleming as the discoverer of how bacterial molds growing on bread could cure a variety of diseases. Most witnesses are. Then the questions ask about the witnesses' familiarity with the ways in which the other physicians at St. Mary's Hospital fought against him, disregarded his far-fetched ideas, tried to get him fired, and how for ten years when Fleming sat down for lunch, his colleagues in the hospital lunch room would move away to another table. The questions then move to explore how experts like the one testifying can be confident and yet so wrong, and how if such people had succeeded, penicillin would have been stopped or substantially delayed from keeping millions of people alive.

When expert witnesses are confronted with such questions, a first internal reaction ought to be satisfaction: satisfaction because attacks on the whole profession signify that the attorneys have been unable to damage the testimony proper and satisfaction because the attorneys who use the technique are grasping at last straws.

A first way of responding is to decline the invitation to be expert on Semmelweiss or Pasteur or Fleming, or the treatment of President Garfield, or the historically wide acceptance of the Szondi Test, or whatever the historical disaster may be. The witness may wish to decline with this answer:

"I am not a historian, so I cannot testify as an expert about the circumstances that surrounded this discovery at this point in time. There are experts in the history of medical sociology who might be able to assist the court better if information about Ignaz Semmelweiss is needed."

Witnesses may opt for discussing historic hysteric events with a calm and objective overview, saying,

"Such medical behaviors by the profession are as shocking to consider today as they were a century ago. Semmelweiss is respected as great pioneer and innovator."

Finally, when the attorneys move to the conclusion about how all current experts, like the present witness, may well be wrong too, the witness should move to positive affirmations of the clinical findings or of the current state of the field of knowledge. An example of the former would be,

"Whatever may have happened in Austria 130 years ago, my clinical examination of Ms. Jones has left me with no doubt whatsoever that she is going to be handicapped as an employee and as a mother for the foreseeable future."

An example of the affirmation of the current state of knowledge is,

"I am proud and pleased to be part of a profession that has substituted scientific knowledge and professional effectiveness for the dreadful myths and poor care of the past century. Each of us should be grateful we live in an era in which good care has been developed and in which we are free from the scientific and medical superstitions that preceded us."

THE MAXIM: *The historic hysteric gambit is an indication that nothing else has worked for the attorney. Respond with poise, either declining to discuss the historical events or dismissing them as obsolete and not applicable.*

❧ 30 ❧

How You Know What You Know

THE QUESTION WAS WHETHER A MILDLY RETARDED YOUNG man had been able to understand the Miranda warnings. The psychologist who had been asked to evaluate the man normally did not do such work. However, the judge had asked her as a personal favor to conduct this evaluation, and in turn, she had called me for advice.

Her idea was to conduct a full psychological evaluation, the kind she would do with any client. What she asked me was how to assess his awareness of Miranda rights. We talked about the Grisso (1981) research into juveniles' abilities to understand Miranda rights through their vocabulary and other means of measuring understanding. Eventually, she had a solid plan for proceeding with her assessment.

The issue goes further than this case and this issue. Every time an expert is asked to become involved in a legal matter, the question can arise in court and should arise in the expert's mind: "How do you know what you know?" A lucid link should exist between the conclusions and the means of reaching those conclusions. Experience or education are never sufficient answers by themselves. The real question is exactly what and how professional skills, training, or expertise were used to come to these particular conclusions.

Assume that the issue before the court was the degree to which an injured man could resume employment and that an expert testified that in five years, up to fifty percent of his employment skills could be regained. The attorneys should ask about the expert's knowledge about five-year follow-ups and about the standards and actuarial assessment data that were applied to come up with the fifty percent figure.

The experts also need to ask the same question, but not only for self-protection in court. Rather, the reason should be to ensure that accountable methods are involved. Without such a foundation, the expert may be vague, uncertain, and not responsible in this legal role.

THE MAXIM: *From the earliest stage of legal activity, be certain to have mastered the foundations of your knowledge and role.*

❄ 31 ❄

Humor

IS IT OKAY TO BE FUNNY WHEN YOU testify? Would it be offensive to be witty? Humorous? To joke? To laugh?

A general principle to follow in deciding whether to joke is to be sure to respect the dignity of the courtroom. Trials are serious events about which people have strong feelings. The witness who is funny may be seen as disrespectful and irreverent.

Furthermore, much humor is unkind. Many jokes take the form of ridicule or disguised hostility. Courtroom humor has the potential for being the equivalent of laughing at someone slipping or falling. A few years ago I was involved in a case in which a guest was shot and seriously injured while staying at a Holiday Inn. At that time, the Holiday Inn national advertising slogan was "The best surprise is no surprise." Suppose, in the course of testifying, I had speculated, tongue in cheek, that the last thing the assailant said before firing his pistol was "surprise." Of course, I did not. Such a remark would have been uncalled for and cruel. Yet, under the tension of the courtroom scene and the performance of giving testimony, witnesses sometimes make equally strained and tasteless efforts at humor and tension release.

I have seen expert witnesses who are witty and acerbic testify with their natural acerbic wit. Their credibility is usually harmed because they are showing an incongruent form of pleasure in these somber proceedings. Judges and juries often dislike these people for the same reasons we dislike smugness; these are emotion blends in which the mixed message is uncomfortable. Consider the adverse consequences of a witness replying to an attorney's challenge to an answer by saying that "only a person with a total vacuum between his ears would not understand what I have been saying."

Yet, humor does have a place in the courtroom. Gentle humor can make the witness seem more human. I sometimes use a mild self-mocking humor. If an attorney asks me why I do not know a particular research study, I may reply in a confident voice that "not only do I not know that study, but there many other studies I haven't read. You have no idea how much I don't know."

For humor to work in the courtroom, it cannot be sharp-edged, brittle, or cutting, Rather, it must be good-humored, which means it should be kind, comfortable to everyone, and presented without defensiveness or rancor. Even then, good humor is acceptable only in moderation. Nobody wants Bozo the Clown on the witness stand.

THE MAXIM: *If you are humorous at all on the witness stand, keep it gentle, good-natured, and infrequent.*

✢ 32 ✢

The Idealism Hazard

I WAS EXHAUSTED. FROM FIRST THING IN THE morning until the end of the work day, I had evaluated a boy's training school and then had been subjected to a grueling deposition about my evaluation for the five hours following. I was tired, hungry, and struggling to pay attention. The attorney for the other side then asked a question that pushed aside my weariness and sent a jolt of energy through me.

"You have indicated the problems in this school," the attorney said. "Now tell us how, ideally, such a school should be run."

Oh, my! The ideas bubbled through me and out in a gush. Respect for the dignity of the kids, an opportunity for the boys to be both free and responsible, and staff who were excited and positive and growing were some of my responses. For thirty minutes I carried on. I then realized what I had been doing. Instead of staying with the assigned task of addressing *minimum* standards for care of these boys, I was painting a personalized, idealistic picture of what such a school should be in the best of all possible worlds.

The consequences of my actions were to move away from sound, accepted foundations of minimum standards. After all, in class-action suits against institutions, as well as in all malpractice and negligence lawsuits, the issue is whether the defendants have provided services or practices that are at least adequate by consensual professional criteria. The law understands, as we do, that not all professionals are outstanding nor all institutions superb. Furthermore, defining what is *minimally* acceptable for the professions has usually been the product of long deliberations. No such standards have been developed for ideal clinicians or perfect schools.

Thus, when experts testify about their idealistic beliefs, they move into a personalized, subjective area. Defending their beliefs as consensual becomes difficult. Furthermore, such testimony can portray the experts as starry-eyed, unrealistic dreamers whose heads are in the clouds, far above the concerns of the ordinary practitioner.

In my deposition, if I had been alert and wise, I would have answered quite differently. My response should have been, "My assessment was not of this school's progress toward any idealized concept. Rather, I evaluated the degree to which the school met minimum standards of care, and in each of the areas I have noted, the school fell far short."

The idealism hazard is not simply that witnesses can get distracted from their task. The hazard is also that they can be seen as essentially out of touch with the basic and realistic conditions at hand. Thus, the surgeon from a major urban medical center should not be condescending toward typical rural medical care because new, expensive technologies are not available. In malpractice, negligence, and class-action suits alike, the charge to the witness is to describe the bottom-line level of adequate services, not the pie-in-the-sky hopes and aspirations of the witness for infallible delivery of perfect services.

THE MAXIM: *When minimum professional standards are the issue, do not become a visionary advocate of idyllic and rarely attainable services.*

❧ 33 ❧

Intimidation

THE CONSIDERABLE COURTESY AND RESPECT MOST ATTORNEYS SHOW toward most expert witnesses is predictable. Sometimes the deference seems to be too much, more than we merit by our positions and work. Yet, every now and then, occasions arise in which one finds attorneys who are deliberately nasty in depositions or while questioning experts on the witness stand or in informal contacts. On these occasions, they attack, bluster, and threaten the opposing witnesses. The attorneys' voices rise to near yelling, their demeanor is hostile, the tone of their questions may overflow with cynicism.

Why would these atypical attorneys even act this way? I have three hypotheses. The first is that some of these attorneys are fundamentally abrasive in nature and act this way in most settings. They are probably short with their clerks, impatient with their secretaries, and—to use one of my favorite southernisms—*ugly* with opposing counsel. They try to intimidate witnesses because intimidation is part of their characteristic style.

The second hypothesis is that these attorneys have developed a mental set that, when in the adversarial role, they need to be truly adversarial. They undergo a malevolent transformation in the deposition room because television dramas and their own social expectations pull out of them an exaggerated display of the indignant attorney. This hypothesis holds that the attorneys are acting this way deliberately in part but also because the situation elicits it.

My third hypothesis is that such efforts to intimidate are planned and purposeful, and are seen most frequently in cases in which the weight of the evidence is hopelessly against the attorneys. In the deposition, without the calming authority of a judge present, these attorneys choose to test the strength of character and ideas of witnesses. The accusations and unpleasant questioning are designed to shake the witnesses and to instill anxiety if the case goes to trial. Witnesses who have undergone aggressive and personal barrages during depositions are often distressed; in those instances, the aim of shaking the witnesses is indeed attained. Such purposeful intimidation also takes place occasionally during trials.

These three hypotheses are not mutually exclusive. Rather, it is likely that all three motives can exist simultaneously.

How should witnesses cope with attorney intimidation? A helpful description of taking one's time in answering is presented elsewhere in this book. However, some further suggestions are in order. When my children were young and speaking loudly and yelling at the breakfast table, I used to talk quietly and evenly with them. They would hush up instantly. Similarly, in depositions and on the rarer occasions of intimidation on the witness stand, I lower my voice so that my calm is juxtaposed in sharp contrast to the stridency of the questions.

At other times I carefully restate the questions to sort out the content from the attack. I may say,

"So what you are asking me is whether my not taking a history of Ms. Smith's adolescent years is unusual and an indication of a lack of comprehensiveness on my part?"

If the attorney acquiesces that I have heard the question accurately as I restate it in neutral terms, I am more in control. I then can go on to answer the question in reassuring terms, such as,

"Every time I take a case history, I select the most relevant areas of the client's life on which to focus. Nobody can take a totally comprehensive history because a huge clutter of irrelevant information about meals, clothing, and so on would be wastefully accumulated. The case history that I did take was designed to explore *exactly* the part of the Ms. Smith's life I needed to be able to draw my clinical conclusions."

In depositions or in the corridors outside of the courtroom, some expert witnesses use clinical skills with intimidating attorneys, treating them as angry clients would be treated in therapy. The attorneys can be told, "I notice you are raising your voice a lot now" or "Are you okay? You seem to be losing control." Attorneys tend to back off quickly when hearing these comments, particularly if they are acting out of the patterns observed in Hypotheses 1 and 2.

These latter suggestions lead to an actual instance I had of dealing with an intimidating attorney. The rule excluding witnesses from the courtroom had been waived and I had been watching a cross-examination of a psychologist friend. The attorney was fierce, pushing, insulting, and reprimanding my friend. My friend, who is an excellent psychologist, did not do well. He stammered and became uncertain about his clinical conclusions.

During the recess after my friend's testimony and before my testimony, I ran into the cross-examining attorney in the hallway. We chatted briefly and then I told him,

"You were truly unpleasant with George on the witness stand. I want you to know that if you try that with me, I will punish you severely up there."

To this day I do not know what prompted me to threaten him like that. It is not my way. However, the attorney smiled weakly, muttered something, and moved away. When I testified, his cross-examination was long but very superficial and impeccably polite.

THE MAXIM: *When attorneys try to intimidate,
respond with controlling answers,
proper manners, and clinical reflections.*

❧ 34 ❧

Just Before the Court Appearance

IN THAT LAST HOUR BEFORE TESTIFYING IN COURT, I get a little nervous, and so do most witnesses I know. My mouth gets a bit dry. Sometimes a small but noticeable tremor appears in my hands. A little queasiness may jiggle my stomach. Although these signs almost always fade away when I actually take the stand, they nevertheless can be unpleasant. There are some positive things one can do to minimize such discomfort.

A routine first step is to be in touch with the attorney who has called you and, equally important, the attorney's secretary, about the speed at which the case is progressing. I am fine with rearranging my schedule if I am going to testify. However, I get irritated if I have had to cancel or postpone appointments and then sit in the witness room for hours waiting to be called. It is no consolation for me to remember that courts have different time needs than I do. I know that my impatience at what seems like geological time (in which events are measured in decades and centuries) does not serve me well; once I am antsy and irritated at waiting, I am likely to be a less effective witness.

Once in Puerto Rico I was called to the stand, but before I

could testify at all, opposing counsel requested and received a one-day adjournment to prepare further for me. The case had been going on for years, and opposing counsel by then had had my report in their hands for 18 months, so I guessed that it was not a postponement for substantive reasons. The next day, when I actually testified, I had gone through an extended period of long-distance calls, re-arranging classes, appointments, clients, and flight schedules. I was annoyed! As a result, for the first part of a full day of testimony, I was off-balance and less persuasive. Later, with scheduling events behind me and out of my mind, I did well.

In the witness room while waiting to testify, some particular steps can make the time feel well spent and the witness better prepared. One suggestion is to bring work that is important to do. Spending this waiting time in a productive venture on either paper-work, writing tasks, or business or enjoyable reading means that a certain element of self-esteem will have been enhanced by the feeling of accomplishment. Another suggestion is to use the time for reviewing case materials related to the testimony. If the material is not current in your memory, this time can be a useful refresher. A third but related suggestion is to use the waiting time to memorize by rote factual aspects of the case. Jurors and judges are impressed by witnesses who can recite from memory the exact times, dates, and details of an assessment. Such a recitation makes the listeners think that the witness has an absolute mastery of the case.

For big cases (actually, in a perfect world, for all cases), the memory and review tasks should have been completed in advance. Relaxing and clearing your mind can be a preferred preparation under these conditions. Tom Grisso (personal communication, November 1990) wrote to me about how he goes about relaxing as his preparation:

> I usually arrange to cut myself off from normal business so that I can get my head together. By that time, however, I don't worry about "rehears-ing." I take a walk, or stop at a favorite place for breakfast on the way to court. For me it's very

important that I be alone at those times. I'm not aware of any need to get "psyched up"; it's more a matter of spending some time tuning out the customary activities of work, so that I can arrive at court relatively uncluttered and properly focused.

Once in St. Louis I did not do the above. I worked right up to 12:30 (the hearing was to be at 1:30), then I had so little time left for lunch that I accepted an invitation to join a couple of colleagues who were bringing in Mexican from a fast-food. Now feeling quite rushed, I grabbed a wonderful thing locally called a "Macho Burrito" and took a bite, whereupon a goodly amount of beans and greasy chorizo squirted out the other end and down my necktie. (The necktie is an essential part of the uniform for me.) Rushing to the bathroom, I discovered that I could not remove the evidence, but I found a way to retie the necktie so that the stains couldn't be seen (requiring that the out-facing part of the tie come down only about half-way to my belt—which was okay with the coat buttoned—and the other end of the tie down to my knees—which was okay when I tucked it into my pants). But now my hands were shaking so greatly that I could not tie it. So a friend did it for me, reducing me in fantasy to age 6 when my father used to do the same. Feeling infantile and incompetent, and with little time to spare, I rushed out to my little '72 VW bug, almost flooded it, drove wildly to the court building, then couldn't find a parking space nearby, causing me to have to run some distance.

Like so many times when an expert witness fears that a catastrophe seems to be about to thunder down, this story has a good ending. The hearing was postponed, and Tom did not have to testify at all. I will not give in to the temptation to write a maxim here about avoiding Macho Burritos (or anything else macho) before testifying, and instead I offer the following:

THE MAXIM: *Explicitly relax or engage
in productive work just before
your court appearance.*

❧ 35 ❧

The Language of Testimony: 1. General Principles

TESTIFYING IN COURT CAN PROMOTE A SHARPENED SENSITIVITY to many aspects of one's behavior, including to the words actually being used to communicate particular ideas. The persuasive witness (as well as the nonpersuasive witness) has observable language patterns. William O'Barr (1978) studied five widely used trial practice manuals from which he identified many speech characteristics associated with persuasive witnesses. Some of these characteristics are relevant to this discussion. The witnesses who are *not* persuasive and *not* convincing are said to show the following behaviors on the witness stand.

- They are overly talkative.
- They exaggerate.
- They are angry or antagonistic.
- They are overdramatic and this seems phony.
- They are extremely slow in answering.
- They overqualify what they say.
- They use unfamiliar words.
- They use hackneyed, conventional analogies.

In contrast, persuasive witnesses were found to show the following opposite verbal behaviors.

- They neither talk too much nor too little.
- They are calm and poised.
- They are neither too quick nor too slow in answering.
- They use narrative, smoothly flowing statements.
- They use original analogies and personal descriptions.

O'Barr went on to explain how attorneys should act to elicit these positive behaviors in their witnesses. My suggestions that follow restate some of the O'Barr (1978) principles so that they may be used by witnesses. Let me start with his first point, which advises attorneys to personalize their own witnesses. My suggestion is

1. *Personalize your own testimony.* The more you are perceived as a real person, albeit with special knowledge, the more favorably you will be received. However, the ways in which witnesses allow themselves to be known should never be gratuitous just for personalization of testimony. Rather, statements that reveal and humanize witnesses should follow the natural contours of the testimony.

O'Barr advised that attorneys try to vary the format of the questions. My parallel advice is as follows:

2. *Vary the format of your answers.* If the same sentence structure is repeated, your audience is not able to pay attention as well. Avoid repetitive use of simple sentences with formats such as, "The defendant completed all of the tests." Sometimes use the dependent clause of complex sentences in the first half and sometimes in the second half of a sentence. Be sparing with phrases that serve as prefaces, such as "It is indeed true that. . . ." Mix long and short answers. Vary the rhythm and pace of your answers.

3. *Look for opportunities to give fairly long, narrative answers during cross-examinations.* Although the opportunity to explain during cross-examination may be denied by skilled questioners, alert witnesses can usually find chances to explain apparent inconsistencies or to correct misleading impressions.

4. *Use pronouns purposefully.* When you make a statement that is founded on common experience and understandings, either

in the profession or among people in general, say "we." That is, say "We know that the frustrations of work and the pressures of being in severe pain can lead us to act and think in ways very different from our ordinary patterns." As noted, "I" personalizes statements. "We" emphasizes accepted and general viewpoints.

A concluding observation about language usage is drawn from Danet and Kermish (1978), who pointed out that most advice about courtroom questions and answers is presented in writing, (i.e., in the form of written language). Yet, the substance is spoken language, and spoken language differs qualitatively from written language. When writing, opportunities exist to polish and rethink. In spoken language, nonverbal communication affects the outcome, and the persuasion process is not always visible from written transcripts. The very best testimony reflects a mastery of the spoken sentence in the trial situation and knowing how to be subtle while still presenting testimony that is cogent and organized when transcribed into a typed record.

THE MAXIM: *Effective language usage comes about when the witness personalizes answers, varies the format, uses narrative well, and produces convincing spoken and transcribed testimony.*

❧ 36 ❧

The Language of Testimony:
2. Fluent Testimony

WHO IS IN CONTROL DURING THE CROSS-EXAMINATION is a question that may have no clear answer. Sometimes an attorney will feel in control, and the witness being cross-examined will also feel in control. At other times, neither attorney nor witness feels clearly in control. Witnesses accurately see much of the content and some of the feeling of the cross-examination coming from the examining attorneys. Gentle questions often evoke gentle answers. Fierce questions may evoke either fierce replies or submissive behaviors. Yet, a number of means exist for witnesses to promote their own preferences for the outcome of the cross-examination. One of these means is the use of specific speech techniques.

Cooper and Cooper (1985; Hill, 1989) have described some of these techniques as *fluency-initiating gestures* (FIGs). These FIGs have been successfully applied to aiding young professionals, executives, and stutterers when they speak in pressure-cooker situations. Four techniques have relevance to courtroom testimony:

1. *Vary the loudness.* People quickly adapt to speech that is at a fixed level of loudness. For witnesses with unusually loud or soft voices, the problem is particularly serious. Speak louder and softer at different times so the jury and judge will not drift away into private reveries. Make the loudness of your testimony a specific area of personal control.

2. *Speak slowly.* When anxious, people typically talk too fast and feel that this speed of talking is not within their control. Speaking slowly helps, and this goal is achieved by pronouncing key words syllable by syllable.

3. *Stress syllables.* Closely related to slow speech is the deliberate change in pitch or volume in pronouncing syllables. Howard Cosell, Paul Harvey, and President Kennedy are examples of individuals who dramatized their public speeches by stressing syllables. All three individuals developed a rhythm that grabbed and held their audiences' attention.

4. *Ease into your breath pattern.* When being taught to shoot a pistol or taught to become a photographer with hand-held cameras, students are instructed to breathe in, begin to exhale, and then to hold their breath and depress the trigger or shutter. That point in the exhalation allows the greatest calmness and control. In the same sense, witnesses should get the stream of exhaled air moving before responding. Under these conditions, witnesses clearly feel more in control of their breath and words.

The place to practice these techniques is not on the witness stand but with a tape recorder. These FIGs are fairly easily learned and are best used if they are overlearned.

Many witnesses already use some of these FIGs; if this is the case, simply being aware of them and their place will be sufficient. For witnesses who find themselves anxious and not effective, practicing these FIGS may contribute to a positive outcome on the witness stand.

THE MAXIM: *Gain control of fluency on the witness stand by speaking slowly, stressing syllables, easing into your breath pattern, and varying the loudness of your speech.*

❧ 37 ❧

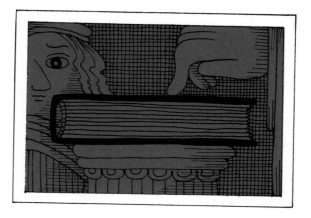

The Learned Treatise Gambit

A S PART OF ATTEMPTING TO UNDERMINE THE CREDIBILITY of expert witnesses, attorneys sometimes present a scientific or professional publication to testifying experts. This learned treatise typically contradicts the experts' knowledge, methods, or conclusions. The publication can take the form of a journal article, a book chapter, a book, an accepted set of standards or taxonomies, or even a newspaper clipping of statements by an authority.

The attorneys' key step is asking if the experts will accept the author or journal or book as a recognized source of professional knowledge. When the author is nationally known or the book a frequently used text, the unsuspecting witness usually agrees. The expert is quickly confronted with a quote or section from the source that explicitly differs from an important part of the witness's own testimony; the witness then (sometimes breathlessly and weakly) tries to reconcile the differences. It is hard to look good when the professor who trained you or the president of your national association is quoted as saying that your basic data—say clinical interviews—are unreliable, invalid, without dependable norms, and idiosyncratic to the individual clinician.

Two options are available when confronted with this ploy. I draw here on the suggestions of Norman Poythress (1980). The first option is to decline absolutely all such acknowledgments of others' expertise unless you have a thorough, ready mastery of the documents or the writings of the expert and do indeed agree with everything in them. Such mastery is rare; this advice, in fact, means declining nearly all of the time. Such refusals to accept these sources or distinguished figures as expert requires great willpower. Consider these examples: The incredulous attorney asks, "You mean to tell this court that you think you know more about clinical interviewing than Harry Stack Sullivan?" Or the question may be, "Isn't the *American Journal of Psychiatry* the most prestigious, most read, most cited, and most respected journal in your field?"

At these times, the witness must not yield to the feeling of being caught as pompous, ignorant, and fraudulent. Instead, a collected demeanor and a response affirming one's opinions and integrity are in order. In response to the first question, the witness might reply, "I cannot speak at all for the writings, experiences, and knowledge of Harry Stack Sullivan." To the second question, the witness might respond, "With over 700 journals and 40,000 articles published every year in my field, no one journal and no one article is by itself important."

If the attorney persists, which is common, the expert may begin to come across as evasive or out of touch with the literature and with important scholars. For that reason, the expert should be prepared to address the key issues and sources. Within the mental health professions, one frequent challenge to diagnostic accuracy is made by attorneys presenting the Rosenhan (1973) treatise, "On Being Sane in Insane Places." On its surface, the Rosenhan article seems to suggest that psychiatric diagnosticians are easily fooled. However, discussions of the weaknesses of the Rosenhan study (these were relatively untrained psychiatric residents making diagnoses from ten-minute interviews) and the limitations on its generalizability (no knowledgeable clinician believes the Rosenhan findings apply to detailed, full diagnostic evaluations for forensic clients) can be responsive, successful replies.

A few approaches within the learned treatise ploy are sufficiently common that they merit individual comment. I describe four approaches, along with suggested tactics for the witnesses.

1. The attorney reads a statement from an expert source that contradicts your testimony. The solution is to ask to see the document from which the attorney is reading. Norman Poythress told me about a time he was being questioned about possible medication effects on the results of an evaluation. The attorney read from the *Physicians' Desk Reference (PDR)* that the medication in question caused hallucinations, delusions, and seizures. Norman asked to see the *PDR* and noted emphatically that the lawyer had omitted one word; the *PDR* stated that the medication *rarely* caused hallucinations, delusions, and seizures. This observation thus destroyed the attorney's argument.

2. The attorney asks you to respond to a piece of an article or book handed to you. Usually, sections of the treatise have been underlined and you are asked to read them aloud. The best tactic is to demur, explaining that although you could indeed read it aloud, it would have no meaning whatsoever for you unless you had a chance to look at the full context of the article or book and that if the court wished to take a sixty-minute recess, you would be pleased to do just that. That offer is an easy one to make. The court never accepts, and it leaves you clearly in control.

3. Every now and then, the cross-examining attorney has drawn on something I have written as the learned treatise that apparently conflicts with my testimony. A foolish move! Nobody is more of an expert on what I have written than I am. If the inconsistency is genuine, and often it is only a seeming inconsistency, I reply honestly about how that was an out-of-date opinion (or an out-of-context paragraph), and how I have learned more since then.

4. Attorneys may use the "prominent author maneuver," in which the writings of a universally recognized authority are explicitly contrasted with the expert's testimony. I like a reply suggested

by Stuart Greenberg, which is, "Are you asking me whether I am generally familiar with the writings of Dr. Prominent or whether I agree with every statement she has ever written? If it is the latter, I don't—and I think most psychologists don't agree with every statement that anyone has written."

THE MAXIM: *Never accept the learned treatise as expertise unless you are master of it.*

✤ 38 ✤

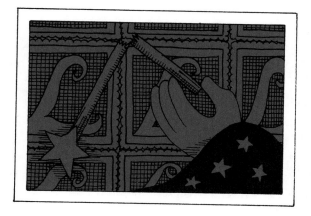

The Limits of Expertise

AN EXPERT WITNESS IS DIFFERENT FROM A LAY witness in several ways. Lay witnesses, which means all individuals not qualified as experts, are allowed to testify only on what they personally have seen and heard (or in special instances, felt, tasted, touched). Expert witnesses are given a privileged status in the courtroom. They are allowed to give opinions.

These are not personal opinions but opinions that come directly from their expertise. For that reason, experts are asked their opinions in phrases that emphasize the nature of the expertise. The questions usually begin, "In your best professional judgment . . ." or "In your best medical opinion . . ." or "Is it your conclusion as a scientist that . . ."

An individual is qualified as an expert on the basis of education, training, skills, or experience. Sometimes a vigorous contest erupts between attorneys about whether a witness truly is an expert. The attorney calling the witness mobilizes all of the impressive available credentials. The opposing side challenges them. The judge ultimately decides. In some states, one need only to have experience "helpful" to the court to be declared an expert.

It is easier to be qualified as an expert in the courtroom than truly to be an expert. When an attorney initially calls on a professional or scientist to be involved in court cases, a careful examination is in order of the nature of the case and the relevance of one's own skills and knowledge. A good rule of thumb is that one should sometimes say no to such requests simply because cases will be so variable that fits between cases and one's credentials will not always be good.

Much professional pain can be saved by saying no early to cases that will be troublesome, and troubling. Trusting your instincts and attending to whether you have genuine mastery of a topic are useful guides.

Equally important is having the courage and insight to let go and withdraw along the way. Attorneys want opinions from experts to buttress their adversarial fisticuffs. Ensuring that one does indeed produce a reasonable proportion of dissenting opinions from the employing side helps ensure an independence and integrity in all court work. Being able to say "I disagree, I cannot support that position" or "That's not my conclusion" to attorneys in these early stages is a double-check that one is maintaining a professional independence.

THE MAXIM: *Agree to be an expert only when genuine expertise is present.*

❦ 39 ❦

Listening Well

THE CROSS-EXAMINATION HAD BEEN GROWING IN FERVOR AND intensity. The attorney was asking difficult questions and the witness was beginning to shift uncomfortably in his chair. The attorney then asked,

"So there are assessment procedures that you did not use, that would have presented more information. Is that correct?"

The witness swallowed his words as he replied, "More or less."

"More or less?" the attorney gloated. "Is it true or isn't it? When you say 'more or less,' is it more true or less true? Please stop being evasive and answer the question!" The attorney paraded back and forth across the courtroom as she continued to berate the witness for the vagueness of his answer.

Two aspects of this exchange call for comment. First, the witness was feeling pressured and tried to deflect the attack by giving an ambiguous reply. Instead of stating an accurate yes, the witness's "more or less" response was a faint effort to resist conceding the point. In cases of this sort, the witness should have fully acquiesced, or fully resisted, or addressed with a powerful reply the ambiguity of the question. More about these particular kinds of responses are discussed elsewhere.

The second aspect of this exchange is that the attorney listened well to the witness's response. Instead of moving on, accepting the weakness of the answer, this attorney clearly heard and leaped on the evasiveness and discomfort of the witness. By making the evasion an issue, the attorney sought to highlight the witness's style of responding as a sign of substantive weakness.

Note what the witness might have said after this flamboyant attack on his answer. He could have retracted the response and said, "The answer is definitely a yes." The witness could have defended the ambiguity of the "more or less" and replied "There were more procedures I might have used, but they were unlikely to have been helpful." Or the witness could have sought to take control by answering, "What I intended to convey is . . ." and to have gone on to a considered explanation using full sentences.

In my illustration, the attorney did what good attorneys should do. She heard the multiple messages in the witness's answer and used that knowledge intelligently. Other attorneys do not listen well.

Some attorneys are excellent at formulating and posing questions but not at truly hearing the responses. These attorneys are recognized by their careful, structured reasoning as they go through their yellow legal pads of prepared questions for the cross-examination. Now and then, I have handled these questions by responding at first in exactly the way the attorney expected. When I see the attorney's attention or gaze drifting to the next question, I continue in the same tone of voice, with content that is still appropriate but that shifts focus somewhat. In other words, I change my answer just enough that the attorney's next question does not quite fit. Everybody in the courtroom realizes that the attorney is no longer precisely on target and the attorney also knows that something is wrong but does not know exactly what has transpired. Compelling cross-examinations change into hesitant ones under such influences.

In the same sense, witnesses who have mastered courtroom

transactions listen with care to what attorneys ask. Most written language and all spoken language is imprecise. In ordinary exchanges, the listener internally fills in with what the speaker apparently means. In cross-examinations, it is possible to listen with sufficient care that the question as literally asked is answered. Suppose the attorney accidently uses a double-negative, perhaps asking, "Is it not true that there still is much you do not know about this person?"

Now if this question were asked as "Is it true that there still is much you do not know about this person?", the witness would answer yes. Thus, with the "not true" in the question, the answer that agrees is no. Another example can be seen when an attorney asked a question about some phenomenon occurring *frequently* when in actuality the phenomenon occurs *sometimes*.

The consequences of such attending to the words in cross-examination questions is that the continuity of the questioning is disrupted. Frequent disrupting of anybody's thoughts is impolite. However, this compulsive attending to actual language usage can rescue a witness from an otherwise difficult situation. Because impoliteness shades readily into pettiness and loss of credibility, witnesses should wait and draw the linguistic sword only when they need the weapon. Listening carefully to the language of questions, which is the foundation of such linguistic grappling, is a skill that witnesses can routinely practice for the occasions when they want it. Perceived expertise is influenced by the precision and professionalism of language; innocuous as well as weighty questions can be used to enhance your credibility.

THE MAXIM: *Listen with care to the wording of the attorneys' questions and use this knowledge in the interests of precision and control.*

❧ 40 ❧

Negative Assertions

THIS DISCUSSION AND THE SECTION ABOUT THE PUSH–PULL reply deal with cross-examination questions that attempt to coerce the witness into agreeing with the attorney. Negative assertions are ways of resisting such attempts. The later discussion of the push–pull method addresses successful ways of agreeing with insistent questions.

When attorneys become pushy during a cross-examination, they hope that witnesses will accept their presentation of facts and conclusions. Usually a series of questions will be asked, generating an increasing momentum for the witnesses to confess that their facts, methods, or conclusions were incomplete or flawed. One way of mastering these questions is through negative assertions.

The term *negative assertions* comes from the assertiveness training literature. Individuals are taught to stand up for their rights, to say no when they feel negative about a request, and to be open and honest with their feelings while respecting the rights of others. An example would be when an acquaintance asks to borrow your car. Responding with a polite but firm no (assuming you do not wish to loan the car) is a negative assertion. In the same sense, asking people in front of you in a theater to be quiet or informing a person attempting to cut into a queue that it is not okay also illustrates negative assertions.

These negative assertions have much in common with courtroom testimony. In both situations, the speaker has to have clarity in what he or she believes and the courage to speak up for that belief. In both situations, the other party will persist unless the message is strong. I have two favorite phrases that help me to be strong and clear on the witness stand: "To the contrary" and "No, that's not it at all." Here is how they work.

"Doctor," the attorney asks, "isn't it true that psychological evaluations of personal-injury impairments always have room for substantial error?"

A weak reply would be, "Well, that's not always so." This reply is vague and nonassertive.

A negative assertion would be, "To the contrary! Psychological assessments provide normative information and scientific foundations compared with what would be casual guesswork for untrained people."

Another negative assertion would be, "Not at all! Nobody can perfectly predict human behavior, but it is simply incorrect to describe it in terms of substantial error."

The reasons that witnesses may have difficulty using negative assertions is that they themselves may be uncertain about the power of their conclusions or because they are intimidated by the attorneys' questions. They need to practice firm ways of saying no. Standing up for themselves will keep them from being transformed into wishy-washy jellyfish moving with the passing current.

It is hazardous to be overly involved in negative assertions. Some witnesses say no to every question that in any way throws doubt on their testimony. These stubborn witnesses are easy to recognize because they give the opposing attorney nothing. Instead, they are supersensitive to the furthest implications of all questions as disputing their findings and as a consequence give a barrage of "no" answers. These knee-jerk reactionaries are not credible. Instead, they come across as being so defensive that judge and jury alike are tentative about accepting their testimony.

THE MAXIM: *When the time is right to disagree with cross-examination questions, do so with strength, clarity, and conviction.*

❧ 41 ❧

Orientation to the Courtroom

AWARE THAT MY PRIOR WORK EXPERIENCE AS A prison psychologist had not prepared me in forensic psychology, I took a leave of absence in 1970 from my teaching position at Southern Illinois University and went as a Visiting Something to the Center for Forensic Psychiatry in Ypsilanti, Michigan. I wanted to learn firsthand about competency and criminal responsibility issues and to spend time with their talented staff. One person I observed, spoke to, and learned much from was Ames Robey, a psychiatrist and the medical director.

Ames was eccentric. He often postured in various ways that demanded people's attention. I visualize clearly the times at restaurants at which he would eat food left over on plates from neighboring tables, explaining to me that the food was perfectly good and that it would only be thrown away anyway. Neither Ames's detractors nor fans would disagree with my view of him as colorful, riveting, and dramatic in court. Everyone in the courtroom listened, really listened, to him.

As an outcome of many discussions, Ames and I wrote an article titled "On Becoming an Expert Witness: Issues of Orientation

132

and Effectiveness" (Brodsky & Robey, 1973). I began to think the article was important when, as part of preparing for this book, I saw the table with our conceptual framework reprinted in several sources. Its importance was confirmed when I noted that occasionally the table was reprinted without attribution as to its source.

Ames Robey and I suggested that expert witness roles call for attitudes, outlooks, and behaviors that are different from most mental health professional roles. These differences are shown in Table 1, in which witnesses who are oriented toward the courtroom and those who are unfamiliar with the courtroom are contrasted.

At the pretrial stage, the courtroom-unfamiliar witness is often tentative and fearful and has little advance knowledge of judicial procedures or of the attorneys' expectations. By contrast, the courtroom-familiar witness has a relevant educational background, understands how expert testimony fits into judicial decisions, is unusually detailed in records, and seeks out early meetings with the attorneys. On the witness stand, the courtroom-unfamiliar witness talks in technical terms, as if for colleagues, sometimes in a detached, uninvolved manner. Such witnesses easily become resentful, anxious, or stubborn. On the other hand, the courtroom-familiar witness speaks clearly and persuasively to judge or jury in terms they understand. The courtroom-familiar expert is sensitive to traps in cross-examination and is not fearful about being cross-examined. These witnesses have no problem in admitting what they do not know and being strong and assertive about what they do know.

After the testimony is completed, the courtroom-unfamiliar witness often leaves feeling alienated and distressed. This witness is sometimes peeved that his or her professional competence and personal worth seemed to have been on trial. The courtroom-familiar witness has known what to expect and typically departs with at least neutral feelings, sometimes quite positive feelings. This witness is usually paid particularly generously as a forensic specialist and seeks to learn from each court appearance as part of improving this base of expertise.

These extremes have been identified for didactic purposes,

Table 1

Comparison of the Courtroom-Oriented and the Courtroom-Unfamiliar Expert Witness

Stage	Courtroom oriented	Courtroom unfamiliar
	Pretrial	
Training	Legal–medical institutes, court clinics, or other training centers. Legal background: sometimes self-taught, by bitter experience	No relevant training
Point of entry of witness into proceeding	Early in legal procedure; extensive pretrial conference with emphasis on appropriate questions to elicit evaluation-related content	Late entry; minimal or no pretrial conference with attorney; minimal or no preparation with attorney on techniques for eliciting opinion
Knowledge of law, evidence, and constitutional privilege	Usually aware; occasionally more so than the particular lawyer in the trial	Usually unaware or minimally informed
Record keeping	Thorough; tends to anticipate cross-examination; exact as to dates, times, places, detail, prior hospital records	Often tends to be variable, imprecise; omits or uncertain of dates, time, etc.
Reaction to subpoena	Minimal emotional reaction; reviews record, calls lawyer, determines basis of subpoena and information desired by lawyer; sets up conferences with lawyer	Distress and anxiety; usually does not call lawyer; no conferences unless requested by lawyer—even then minimal; unaware of legal position
	On the witness stand	
Written report	Clear, concise, equivocal where necessary; avoids legal problems but answers questions raised	Technical language, poorly understood by lay readers; often does not answer legal questions raised

Stage	Courtroom oriented	Courtroom unfamiliar
Target of testimony	Jury or judge	Lawyer or mental health colleagues
Language	Spoken English	Professional terminology
Purpose of testimony	Persuasion; teaching; mild advocacy of his or her findings	"Objective" presentation of clinical information
Testimony process	Steady; consistent; aware of "traps"; concedes to minor points easily	May be badly manipulated; gets stubborn; backs into corner
Reaction to cross-examination	Normal acceptance as routine procedure	Resentment, anger, professional confusion
Setting up rebuttal on redirect examination	Active involvement; awareness of techniques	No activity; unaware of techniques
Posttrial		
Reaction after court findings, especially to distortion of opinion and loss of case by client	Acceptance; learns; reappears in court	Nonacceptance; alienation; reacts by future avoidance
Results of court adjudication	More consistent with expressed view of witness whether opposing testimony is present or not	Less consistent with expressed view, particularly in borderline or contested cases with opposing testimony
Fees	Higher, based on actual time spent in evaluation, reporting, and courtroom time; based on regular private practice fees	Variable, generally low or occasionally unrealistically high compared with regular private practice fee for service time

Note. This table has been modified slightly from the original version by Brodsky and Robey (1973). Copyright © 1973 by the American Psychological Association. Reprinted with permission.

and of course many expert witnesses fall somewhere between the poles. I have lost touch with Ames Robey (are you out there somewhere, Ames?), but he was the quintessential witness familiar with the court setting. And more often than not, I feel pretty much at home there as well.

THE MAXIM: *Effective witnesses are familiar with expected trial procedures, interpersonal transactions, and the dynamics of testifying.*

❧ 42 ❧

Power and Control on the Witness Stand: 1. The Process

I N A SENSE, COURTROOM TESTIMONY IS A STRAIGHTFORWARD task. The witness has information to impart. Attorneys ask questions to bring out this information and then other attorneys ask additional questions to contend with that information and to critique it. Yet, much more than these simple processes also takes place. Attorneys may become dramatic or intense. Witnesses may become emotional and sometimes far less persuasive than they might be under other circumstances. More goes on than obviously meets the eye and ear. Although many concepts may be applied to understanding these transactions, one useful model is thinking of these feelings and events in terms of power and control.

During the direct examination, a cooperative attitude is promoted between witness and attorney. The attorney wants the friendly witness to be convincing, and the power of having the floor is readily shared. The attorney takes all possible steps to give the witness time, attention, deference, and assumptions of correctness.

The cross-examination involves parties with competing

interests. The witness wants to be convincing. The attorney wishes to devalue the witness's conclusions. This conflict takes place on many levels. Questions about the content are asked and answered. However, a more subtle and perhaps equally important level of exchange takes place as a battle for power and control.

If the cross-examining attorney has the witness under control, the attorney will direct the flow of the testimony, accurately anticipate responses, and shape the "feel" as well as the substance of the exchanges. If the witness is in control, the answers will conform to what the witness substantively believes and knows rather than to intimations of the attorney. The witness will accurately anticipate the questions of the attorney and the witness will be unequivocally in control of his or her own feelings.

The struggle for power and control takes place in many ways. Thorough preparation for the cross-examination by either party can make a significant difference in gaining control. Knowledge of the subject under consideration has the same effect. And mastering the psychological links that bind witness to attorney can be extraordinarily helpful.

Attorneys assume control by use of tone of voice, by questions that elicit yes or no answers, by facial expressions, by gestures, by eye contact, by dramatic interpersonal posturing, and by taking the witness to a planned destination, much like leading a reluctant mule down a difficult path. Attorneys at their best are in absolute control. Not only do they know it, but the witness knows it and all of the courtroom observers know it too. The attorney seems to grow in size and to dominate by force of logic or person.

Witnesses have particular difficulty coping when they do not understand what is happening. Whatever they say during cross-examination somehow makes the situation worse, but the witnesses cannot follow why their performance has deteriorated. Witnesses may tend to attribute causes to tricky lawyers or nervousness about testifying. However, witnesses who genuinely follow the unfolding of the cross-examination are in an excellent position to cope with it.

Power and control can sometimes be maintained by

witnesses even when the attorneys attempt to wrestle them away. (In the next three chapters of this book, I describe some of these methods.) It is not necessary to be in control to do well in courtroom testimony, but it is important to not feel controlled, to have the sense of holding your own, and to be at least buoyantly neutral, comfortable with your level of performance. Thus, resisting being controlled is a minimal goal for witnesses and, when successfully accomplished, yields the opportunity to defend your observations and conclusions. Maintaining control is a greater aspiration and is more difficult. If maintained, such control produces a mastery of the courtroom milieu that can be profoundly satisfying.

THE MAXIM: *Cross-examining attorneys will use substantive and psychological means to gain control over witnesses. Witnesses, in turn, need to be free of such control to perform well and feel good about their testimony.*

❧ 43 ❧

Power and Control:
2. Time and the Art of Testifying

I TOOK THE TITLE OF THIS CHAPTER FROM the Robert Grudin (1982) book, *Time and the Art of Living.* I was fascinated with learning about time from Grudin. I gave the book as a wedding present; I sent copies to my sister, son, daughter, and good friends and kept a few copies to give to people when we spoke of time.

As I write of time here, I draw on what Grudin wrote. During difficult moments on the witness stand, the experience of time changes, as Grudin (1982) describes:

> The mind projects its joys and woes so powerfully onto the face of time that changes in mood can all but create new temporal worlds. The negative or painful emotions—guilt, anger, envy, greed, etc.—usually involve a fragmentation of time, a sense of isolation in the present or fixation on some aspect of the past or future. (p. 98)

The emotions felt by attacked witnesses are often anxiety, embarrassment, shame, irritation, or outright anger. These negative emotions cut off the flow back and forth in time, dam up the stream of knowledge into the present moment, and limit the ability to experience the present as part of professional continuity from past to future.

Time seems to be controlled by the attacking attorney. The skilled attorney seems to have complete mastery of the pace at which the interaction unfolds. The attorney asks questions slowly, with languid implications of our ignorance or bias or sloth, or rapidly without pause, our thoughts and ideas tumbling down the steep staircase of which the inquisition is constructed. Grudin (1982) has a section of his book called "Bondage in Time," in which he writes of how we customarily view time as being external to us, something we kill, spend, or waste rather than being internal and within our control. Understanding time as being internal and within our control on the witness stand can transform an odious court appearance into a positive, or least acceptable, time.

Breathing is a way to influence time. The attorney who plods along or shoots machine-gun fast questions is attempting to use time to control. I find that deliberately taking a deep breath before I answer puts me in control of the pace of my replies and sometimes in control of the whole exchange. One or two breaths provide considerable time for thinking through answers and for relaxing too.

I sometimes take more than just a few seconds to think. If the question is unusually provocative, original, or difficult, I truly take time to think before answering. I let the court know I am thinking because this act legitimizes the time I may need. Thus, I visibly demonstrate the signs of thinking. I may take off my glasses and hold the ends in slightly pursed lips. I may put my fingers to my chin and rub but never put fingers to my forehead, which is a distress signal. I may clasp my hands together and gaze off, perhaps with brow furrowed. Looking away from a task at hand is a message that I am thinking. I may look at the ceiling or down at my hands or off to the side. I allow my eyes to unfocus, a universal indicator of a person attending to inner processes. I cease blinking. I lean back until ready to reply, with the leaning back showing a temporal retreat from the engagement with the attorney. When I am almost ready to answer, I lean forward noticeably, which reengages me with the attorney, but I also wait an additional second, signifying how deliberately I have chosen what to say.

These signs are not an act. Otherwise they would not work. Instead, these behaviors should be part of a true consideration of an important issue. Do not give extended thought to questions about your age or about questions that seek repetition of content from your direct examination. Public displays of thought are appropriate only for issues that require thought. Furthermore, after such a thinking pause, all of the courtroom participants will be carefully listening, which is all the more reason to be sure that something thoughtful is offered.

A limit always is present for how long a witness can think, and the limit depends in part on how well the witness is accepted by the judge. In any case, if the witness waits too long, say, more than five, or at the longest, ten seconds, the judge is likely to urge an answer. If that happens, the witness should agree, pause another second to ensure that the answer is not rushed by the judge's demand, and answer.

Giving a persuasive answer while feeling threatened and defensive is, as Grudin (1982) wrote in a somewhat related vein, "like scanning the horizon from a hole" (p. 29). Using time allows the witness to rise at least to ground level and give thoughtful answers.

THE MAXIM: *Take a breath and explicitly think about questions that require thought.*

❦ 44 ❦

Power and Control:
3. Gaze and Eye Contact

INSTRUCTORS OF TRIAL ADVOCACY OFTEN TEACH LAW STUDENTS where to stand during direct and cross-examinations. During the direct examinations, the student lawyers are taught to stand just beyond the jury, so that witnesses will make eye contact with the jurors as well as with the attorney when answering. The goal in the cross-examination is to avert witness eye contact with the jury, and the students are instructed to stand away from the jury. The premise is that the witness will look at the cross-examining attorney while answering and will not maintain the personal credibility with the jury that comes with good eye contact.

These suggestions are founded on a sound principle; we believe people who look us in the eye. Think of the terms in common use that support this principle. We speak of shifty-eyed people, of people who will not look us in the eye as a sign of untrustworthiness. People we do trust are frequently described as steady-eyed, as not afraid to look right at us. Furthermore, direct eye contact can be reinforcing to both parties. I say "can be" because eye contact

143

always means involvement. In loving situations, two people will gaze into each others' eyes so deeply that they may exclude third parties from this private, intimate contact. Eye contact by a hostile stranger can be threatening or challenging. When I am in a large city and strangers try to look me in the eye, I look away most of the time. I know they will be asking me for money or harassing me. Occasionally, I will stare back and become part of a dominance struggle to see who will break off the eye contact first. When I win, I feel a momentary sense of triumph, physical and satisfying.

In the courtroom, eye contact can be part of a positive affiliation for the witness when the witness is speaking to the jury in a personal manner and negative when the witness is captured by the opposing attorney's eye contact during a cross-examination. My operating rule is to try to talk to the jury and to the judge, and to look at them when I talk—up to a point.

If the jury or judge gets the idea that they are being looked at just to persuade them, they will be alienated. For all of us, anyone who attempts to attain an ulterior aim in an interaction will be seen as suspicious. Thus, if the jurors believe that the eye contact is instrumental, in the service of convincing them, the witness is better off gazing in the air. The solution to this dilemma is to look especially at the jury or judge but also at all courtroom participants when answering questions. Looking at observers, the court reporter, the bailiff, all attorneys, and the judge and jury validates looking at the judge and jury.

Looking in this manner is easiest in the direct examination, when the questions are open-ended and when the attorney wants this persuasion to take place. The cross-examination is harder because skilled attorneys will ask closed-ended questions and will seek to coerce witnesses to have eye contact only with them. The attorneys achieve some of this coerced eye contact through the nature of the task itself. Witnesses are like most other people in that they are drawn to look at a questioner when they answer questions. Reciprocal looking is ingrained, even in situations when it is counterproductive.

The witness looks back at the cross-examining attorney and desires all of the nonverbal signs of approval. If the attorney is good, the head nods, the slight raising of the corners of the mouth, and cocking of the head to the side are withheld. The witness may feel unsuccessful as a consequence, no matter how good the response truly is. With yes–no or single-word responses, the witness has little choice. Looking back at the attorney is necessary; otherwise, the witness would come across as rude and inappropriate. However, narrative answers give the witness the opportunity to look at the courtroom participants.

Many witnesses cannot. They are captured by the attorneys asking the questions and continue looking at them, and they react as if they must be responsible to the attorneys. These witnesses act as if they must please the cross-examining attorneys, an impossible task with skilled attorneys. The witnesses are acting normally but ineffectively.

The more effective alternative is to look initially at the attorney as the narrative reply begins and then scan, looking purposefully and in sequence at the jury and others present. This procedure requires going back to look periodically at the attorney so that the attorney is not totally ignored.

The power of this method is seen in attorneys' discomfort. They get nervous. They start to walk around or pace. They try to interrupt answers. One attorney stepped close and juxtaposed his body between my line of vision and the jury. I looked around him. The attorneys need the eye contact as witnesses answer their questions. Taking it away takes power away from them. Just as surely as staring down a stranger at an airline terminal is a dominance victory, so is looking away from an attorney who wants this eye contact.

The knack of answering with brief looks at the attorney and longer eye contact with jurors and others requires practice to do it right. Scanning from one person to another should flow naturally and neither feel like nor look like game playing. The attorney must be disempowered but not ignored. Particular people should be visually identified to talk to during the scanning. Finally, the witness should understand that such eye contact is not a tricky device to win a battle, although it has some of those elements. This eye contact is an earnest means of doing well what brings the witness to the courtroom, that is, to present one's knowledge in a positive means to all of the listeners who are interested.

THE MAXIM: *Look at the jury during narrative answers and avoid being captured in eye contact by the cross-examining attorney.*

❧ 45 ❧

Power and Control: 4. Personal Space

O UR ENVIRONMENTS SHAPE OUR BEHAVIORS FAR MORE THAN most of
us realize. Because we adapt to the relatively constant demands of our daily environments, we do not recognize their pulls
and tugs. New surroundings alert us to such demands and the courtroom environment has its own peculiar demands. It is a theater of
sorts, with jury and observers as the audience not permitted to
participate. The actors are the speakers, judge, attorneys and witnesses, the plaintiffs and defendants. The judge is the director of
the unfolding drama as scripted in part by the law.

The physical environment of the courtroom is both familiar
and unfamiliar: familiar because television, movies, and photographs
have shown hundreds of courtrooms and unfamiliar because this
environment is different from other work settings. For any expert
witness, visiting a new courtroom before the trial or personal
appearance can make the courtroom less alien. Simply sitting in
advance in the witness chair, doing nothing active, can let the surroundings become familiar without the anxiety associated with being
on the spot as an expert witness. Individuals who have sat passively
for a while before their testimony, when the court is not in session,

tell of initial nervousness, which gradually lessens and prepares them for being in the same seat during the trial.

The witness box itself can elicit discomfort and reduced effectiveness during testimony. Many witness boxes have seats bolted to the floor, inadequate shelf space for records, squeaky microphones, and high privacy shields that reduce short people to child-like straining to lift themselves and see as they testify. I am tall and I find some witness boxes constructed to make me feel small as well. Low chairs prompt that feeling, and so does the placement of witness boxes at the side and base of towering judicial benches.

One more element contributes to the sense of physical and psychological smallness. The attorneys speak while standing. The only other person with whom the witness communicates is the judge, who is always seated high above everyone in the courtroom. The witness is looking up, an act that is associated with submissive behaviors. Dogs, wolves, professors, and business executives all understand that the dominant animal looks down at the one lower on the pecking order, and this knowledge is so ingrained in basic animal instincts in human beings that conscious efforts are necessary to overcome it.

One step for combating environmentally produced submissiveness is posture. Ineffective witnesses stay low in the box and chair; some witnesses shrink even lower as a cross-examination progresses, slouching into positions that hint of hiding. Effective witnesses sit with spine straight and body erect, seeming to rise above the chair, box, and attorneys. A good strategy is to lean forward occasionally toward the attorneys, judge, and jury so that the reaching out physically can set the mood for reaching out substantively.

Remember that perception of size is influenced by the attitude of the person involved. Everybody knows of individuals who appear much taller than they are. One friend of mine is 5'4" but says that few people believe she is that short (I apologize to all readers who are less than 5'4" and who do not consider themselves short). Because she carries herself with such interpersonal power, both friends and strangers assume she is much taller. That enhanced size perception is available to everyone who sits or stands tall and carries his or her body with a message of strength and dominance. The lesson is that such felt potency is readily available, but you do have to transcend the encapsulated feeling that is produced by the court-room environment. One specific example may help illustrate the process.

Attorneys in federal courts are restricted to asking questions behind the podia. In many state and local courts, attorneys are allowed to move about freely. Now and then, attorneys will seek to intimidate witnesses by standing very close to them, sometimes leaning their faces near the witness's face as they press forth with aggressive questions. This intrusion into personal space makes the witness feel small. The invisible bubble of private space around one's physical being has been invaded. At these times, witnesses may act weak and speak ineffectually.

My advice is to move forward, to lean toward the attorney, and then to answer. Leaning forward puts the witness in charge and negates the invasion of personal space. In fact, the attorney who attempts this maneuver will usually move as close as his or her body boundaries will permit. The witness leaning forward thus invades the attorney's private space, and attorneys quickly back off, sur-rendering the space and the minibattle to the witness. At this point, the quality of the cross-examination questions often changes, be-coming less strident and more tentative. The witness has used per-sonal space as a vehicle for power and control.

THE MAXIM: *Make the courtroom environment familiar and create an opportunity for control by sitting tall and owning personal space.*

❦ 46 ❦

The Primary Source Gambit

J AMES V. MCCONNELL BECAME FAMOUS FROM HIS RESEARCH with flat-
worms, from editing the half-comic journal *The Worm Runners
Digest*, and from his splendidly readable introductory psychology
textbooks. He was virtually unnoticed in psychology for his penetrat-
ing analyses for attorneys on how to examine expert witnesses. Here
I draw on one of his best observations, an approach he called the
"primary source gambit."

McConnell (1969) assumed accurately that few experts have
read the original articles or books in which fundamental scientific
discoveries appeared. Instead, experts read texts or secondary sources, which always have some element of interpretation or distortion,
if nothing else, by exactly what aspects of the original studies they
emphasize. Thus, McConnell urged attorneys to select the appropriate moment and to begin a series of questions such as the
following:

> "Doctor, . . . were you the first person to
> report this very interesting scientific finding?"
> [No.]
> "Who did make this finding first?"

"Just when and where were these findings first published?"

"When was the last time you read this paper?"

"With such an important point as this, don't you think you should have read the original?"

"Isn't it true that many errors creep into textbooks?"

"Don't you owe it to the jury to have been diligent enough to have gone straight to the original source?" (McConnell, 1969, p. 64)

When this gambit works, expert witnesses find themselves admitting their ignorance and lack of full preparation. The good expert is a prepared expert and should know the major original sources. However, even the complete expert will not have read, say, Alfred Binet in French. Some good responses include,

"Not only have I not read Binet in the original French articles and books, neither has any other psychologist I know. We are much more interested in what these ideas mean for our research and our clients today than what they meant for retarded youngsters in Paris a hundred years ago."

This reply clarifies the current context of knowing such information as well as the case for not knowing an original source (it is not relevant). Look at two other responses to primary source questions:

"Of course, many errors creep into text books. It is one of the reasons those of us who read and use them insist on frequent revision."

"A diligent psychologist here means being absolutely thorough and conscientious in examining the defendant and has nothing to do with resurrecting the long-revised and functionally obsolete writings of a long-dead scholar."

The good attorney will persist. In these cases, the expert witness must remember that these primary-source inquiries are essentially distraction techniques not dealing with the substance of the testimony. The expert witness is best off staying relaxed and easy and letting these questions wash on by.

THE MAXIM: *If you do not know primary sources, worry not. Instead, stay with current knowledge and clinical conclusions.*

Probes for Guilt and Shame

ONE FORM OF AGGRESSIVE QUESTIONING IN THE CROSS-EXAMINATION is probing for the development of feelings of guilt and shame in expert witnesses. Feelings of guilt are induced by making the witnesses feel that they did not perform some professional act that they should have. Feelings of shame are induced by leading witnesses to feel or, even worse, admit that they did something they should not have. Here are some guilt-inducing questions drawn from John Tracy's (1957) book, *The Doctor as a Witness*, and some possible replies.

"Doctor, when you examined the plaintiff on July 22nd of this year, was your examination a complete and thorough one?"

Uh-oh, the witness thinks, did I leave out something? Is this attorney going to nail me for omitting some part of my examination? I wish I had more time to do it right. These insecure feelings are intensified if the attorney continues to build on such inquiries.

"And, doctor, I suppose you took a comprehensive history?"

"Doctor, your notes are fairly complete, are they?"

Witnesses sometimes become obviously defensive at this point. They may overexplain the limitations of all examinations.

Some witnesses talk fast and loud, and deny any possible omissions in their examinations, histories, or notes. My suggestion is not to rush to defend yourself. After all, the attorney is still setting up an argument, and so many attorneys are inept at wrapping up arguments that witnesses need not try to win this battle before the opposing weapons are visible.

Instead, witnesses are better off responding with accurate, pointed answers stated in a confident manner. Here are some illustrative replies:

"Yes. My examination did completely and thoroughly assess Ms. Jones for the psychological effects of the accident." [Note that the examination is not described as complete for all purposes but only for the immediate concern.]

"The history I took comprehensively covered all of the background that needed to be investigated for this client."

"Oh, yes. My notes completely served the purpose for which I took them." [If the attorney asks what that purpose was, the answer might be that they were brief notes to supplement memory.]

A similar process operates for shame-inducing questions. Consider this cross-examination question from Tracy (1957, p. 95):

"Have you ever talked to anyone about this case?"

The witness thinks, Oh, no! I shouldn't have talked to my husband (or wife) about this case. And they are going to find out that I talked for all that time with the attorney who called me. The solution, of course, is to tell the truth.

"Yes, I have. I spoke to Mr. Bailey and I spoke to my husband as well before I came to court."

Some attorneys will follow by insinuating that your attorney told you what to say. This insinuation is handled by explaining kindly that the attorney wanted to know what your testimony would be and wanted to know if the questions the attorney had planned would accurately bring out your results and conclusions.

The guilt and shame probes work with two kinds of witnesses: (a) those who feel much guilt or shame anyway and are ready to generalize the court setting and (b) those who are so threatened by being on the witness stand that they either overexplain or overconfess. These probes do not work successfully against the experienced and secure witness.

THE MAXIM: *Cross-examination probes for guilt and shame are effective only if you respond with guilt and shame. Stay on-task and nondefensive.*

❧ 48 ❧

The Professional Witness

PART OF LEARNING WHO AND WHAT ONE IS as a witness is to learn who and what one is not. For most witnesses this definition by exclusion starts with not being a professional witness, that is, an expert who is often thought of as slick, glib, and suspect because of a specialization in testifying in civil lawsuits for plaintiff lawyers. Nils Nordstrom (1962) has compared what he called the "best witness" with professional witnesses, and he described the professional witness on the stand in these terms:

> Fortified with excess talent in showmanship, supported by inherent brilliance of intellect, and protected by the respect offered the medical profession, it would not be an exaggeration to say that such an individual is practically invincible! Faced by a man who exudes authority, who can describe situations—even operations—*better than the specialist himself,* and who can parry thrusts of cross-examination with the expertness of a swordsman, *most lawyers dare not attack!* Authority of manner, voice, and speech, superimposed on the Hollywood concept of what a

doctor "should look like," is for all practical purposes an unbeatable combination, and attacks on
credentials are easily sidestepped by a smile, or
a word—sometimes even double talk. (p. 53)

A rethinking of our automatic rejection of any and all
semblance to professional witnesses is needed. Although some
professional witnesses are not qualified by experience or training
as substantial experts, and in fact are suspect or outright shady,
others are indeed qualified. Some professional witnesses have
retired or changed emphases in their careers. Others have chosen
the courtroom as a more challenging venue for their skills and
knowledge than the clinic. Most of them are sincere in their beliefs
and self-assured about their opinions. For the typical expert witness
whose primary vocation is elsewhere than the courtroom, the professional witness offers several exemplary traits worth pursuing in the
interests of becoming a better witness. Such professional witnesses
are

- always interesting to watch and hear,
- able to reconfirm statements of their findings from practical
  experience,
- truly abreast of the latest literature,
- skilled at neutralizing vicious cross-examination attacks,
- composed and relaxed.

Finding good models for the witness role is difficult for oc-
casional expert witnesses. They shun an unnecessary trip to the
courtroom as if it were a contagious disease. Instead of grumbling
about the professionals or scientists who spend much of their working time in the courtroom, an expert can gain by going to observe
these talented professional witnesses. Their mastery of the court
drama and role can offer a breadth of ideas about constructive
behaviors for experts to adapt to their own needs.

THE MAXIM: *Talented professional witnesses can model authoritative expertise for other experts.*

❦ 49 ❦

Psychotherapists as Expert Witnesses

TO SOME OBSERVERS, EVERY TIME A MENTAL HEALTH professional takes the oath to tell the whole truth and nothing but the truth, an ethical deceit and a conflict of interest take place. The ethical deceit exists because the relativistic nature of mental health knowledge means that the whole truth never exists. The conflict of interest is a tug of war between professional obligations and roles and courtroom adversarial procedures that seem to deal with selective knowledge and black-and-white characterizations. These same issues become more compelling when a preexisting conflict of interest is present in the form of the witness having served (or currently serving) as psychotherapist of an involved party. This kind of conflict has led to the mental health professional being characterized as a "double agent" (Melton, Petrila, Poythress, & Slobogin, 1987).

Psychotherapists do not want to be expert witnesses in court cases about their clients. Quite to the contrary, therapists view such activities with distaste. From what therapists have told me, if they were given a choice between testifying about their clients or being sentenced to thirty days' imprisonment at hard labor, they would have to think hard to make a decision. Sometimes that very choice is foisted on them (without the hard-labor part); judges have ordered psychotherapists to testify about confidential disclosures by clients or face jail for contempt of court. For the most part, they testify. Occasionally, confidentiality takes absolute priority over the demands of justice and the legal process, and they choose jail.

The most common reason psychotherapists testify is about child custody. They testify about what may be in the best interests of a child client or about parenting skills and adjustment of the parent who is or has been a client. Psychotherapists are also called to give evidence about clients who have filed personal-injury actions, who are criminal defendants, or who are seeking parole or probation. These matters are most easily addressed if the therapist knows at the outset that legal issues will arise. In that case, the therapist can discuss with the client the limits of confidentiality and sometimes can arrange for an independent clinician to assume responsibility for assessment. Most of the time, however, the therapist has few hints that the legal issue will impinge on the therapy and lead to a court appearance.

When the subpoena appears and the therapist is deposed or goes to court, a tension can be created between the obligation to testify with impartiality and the partisanship of caring for the client. Good attorneys exploit that tension with questions such as these:

"Doctor, isn't it fair to say that you did not come forth today on your own but rather had to be subpoenaed to come to court?"

"Would you please tell the court what the responsibility is for a psychotherapist in terms of helping a client achieve a happier and fuller life?" (This is usually followed by a question about whether the client seeking compensation for an injury or custody or freedom from imprisonment would be happier.)

"What does 'therapeutic alliance' mean? Why is it important in psychotherapy?"

"Everything considered, would a psychotherapist's opinion be as detached and objective as that of a clinician who sees the same client only for an assessment?"

This genre of questions is directed at exposing the bias in

favor of the client. Attorneys understand that psychotherapists do not want to testify and attempt to bring that reluctance and ambivalence into the open. The answers by the witnesses should depend on an honest self-examination of their objectivity. If their involvement is more subjective, the client's attorney should know that up-front, and the witness should be prepared to say so (even though the consequence may be a barrage of attacking questions and ugly exchanges). More frequently, the psychotherapist will be in a position to be reasonably objective. If so, here are some replies to the essence of the preceding questions:

"The nature of the therapeutic alliance and caring for the client is always in a professional context. Psychotherapy is not friendship, with all of its personal involvement. Rather, psychotherapy means being able to be both a participant with the client and at the same time a neutral observer. It is to attain just that balance and skill that psychotherapists receive so much training and supervision."

"Psychotherapists have one advantage over clinicians who are just evaluators: They have the chance to see a person over a long period of time, to come to know a person extraordinarily well without the person being defensive or opaque, to really, truly know and understand a person."

Psychotherapists as witnesses should be able to admit to themselves, and to the court if the occasion arises, all of the limitations and conflicts they may experience in testifying. Yet, psychotherapists should equally value their special expertise and information, and should speak to those strengths as well.

THE MAXIM: *It is normal for psychotherapists to be reluctant or ambivalent when testifying about their clients. Testimony should include the strengths of the participant-observer role and the extended opportunities to observe their clients.*

❧ 50 ❧

The Push–Pull

O NE FORM OF PSYCHOLOGICAL WARFARE DURING THE cross-examination is the attorney's effort to put the witness on the defensive. A defensive witness is a less credible witness. The witness who is uncomfortably denying weaknesses in the profession or in his or her own work is less likely to be persuasive than a comfortable, nondefensive witness.

Attorneys' efforts to make witnesses defensive can take the form of questions that identify known flaws in method, background, or inferences. These questions are often more difficult for witnesses when they are presented in an accusatory tone.

A productive way of avoiding defensiveness is to use the push–pull technique (Brodsky, 1977; Brodsky & Poythress, 1985). When the attorneys push, the defensive instinct is to push back, to defend oneself. Defensiveness is seen in grudging admission of flaws and feisty and argumentative replies. I suggest the martial arts philosophy; when the attorney pushes, the witness pulls in the same direction. Consider the following cross-examination questions designed to make witnesses defensive:

"Isn't it true that some people in your field have written that the clinical interview, on which you so depend, is a subjective, unstandardized, and unreliable method?"

The defensive answer would be that clinical interviews are indeed reliable and useful in the witness's own experience. However, that answer would not attend to the question. A push–pull would be,

"My gracious, yes! These people say the clinical interview is absolutely worthless and absolutely useless."

This response makes it evident that the witness knows about these criticisms and is not the least bit flustered or distressed. That poise is communicated to the judge or jury. A few additional illustrations of push–pulls show this process.

"Don't you wonder if you have done everything possible in such a complex evaluation with so many issues?"

"I wonder very much. Even after I go beyond all of the routine and expected procedures, I do wonder what else I might have done."

"When you advise that Rosemary feels secure and loved in the custody of her mother, you are not infallible, are you?"

"Of course not. Nobody is infallible, and I surely am not infallible."

"Isn't it true that you have not published even one article or research study in any journal, anywhere, about your work?"

"Not only have I not published even one journal article, I also have not given any presentations to any professional meetings anywhere."

In the latter case, some witnesses may choose to add that writing articles and making presentations is not what they do, so it should not be surprising that they have not published or presented anywhere.

The push–pull has the effect of making the question part of the witness's general presentation of self. The witness makes the question and the subject his or her own. By embracing the question in an accepting, knowledgeable manner, the witness demonstrates a comfort and mastery of the situation. That comfort and mastery are far more persuasive than any negative implications of the answer.

My style, as seen in the examples just given, is to begin my answer with strong declarative agreement, such as "My goodness, yes!" The strong declarative opening, if said in an assertive and confident tone of voice, has the effect of saying to the cross-examining attorney, with the court listening, "Of course, you empty-headed cretin, everybody knows that!"

Additional examples may be seen in the following three push–pull responses to the question, "Isn't it true that validity of interviews is a serious problem in the mental health professions?"

"Every single one of us in the profession takes very seriously this problem of validity of our interview methods."

"Certainly! I consider the validity issue so important that I consider it carefully in each and every one of my assessments."

"Oh yes. It is not only the validity problem about which we are concerned but also the issues of reliability, objectivity, and standardization."

If the push–pull is seen by the court as a gambit instead of a genuinely felt reply, a rebound effect of negative judgments may occur. As with all techniques, the push–pull works when it fits naturally with the witness's own style, when it is not overused, and when it is offered comfortably and spontaneously.

THE MAXIM: *When the cross-examination question is true but is asked in a pushy and negative manner, consider agreeing strongly.*

❦ 51 ❦

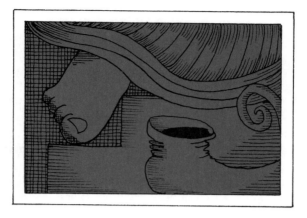

Quiet Moments on the Stand

FEW BATTLEFIELDS ARE CONSTANTLY BOMBARDED BY EXPLODING SHELLS, nor are witnesses on the stand constantly challenged and attacked. Most fears of testifying are quieted as the witnesses find how weak and insubstantial is the cross-examination. The interesting issue in these moments of relative peace (I would never call them serenity) is how to use the moments constructively and positively. For many witnesses, the primary outcome is relief that they had not stepped into a manhole or fallen into a foxhole. Yet, these quiet times are potentially useful as preparation for the more difficult and skilled crosses. I have listed four suggestions for making constructive use of these quiet times.

1. *Anticipate difficult questions.* Before the trial, when you are thinking privately and quietly about your testimony, prepare the most difficult cross-examination questions you can generate. Phrase precisely and write on paper the questions that would accurately and pointedly address the most uncertain aspects of your credentials, objectivity, data, and conclusions. Then, consider how you would handle these questions. This process of assuming the roles of question asker and answerer allows you to move beyond defensive kinds of witness

thinking. An additional nice payoff can result. If you are working later with an attorney in an advisory capacity rather than as a witness, you can be better at helping to challenge other experts' testimony.

2. *Observe with safety.* Unchallenged times on the stand give you a chance to look carefully at courtroom dynamics and processes. It is hard to do so when you are stressed, ducking artillery shells, or throwing back hand grenades lobbed your way. While it is safe, pay attention to the judge, the jury, both sets of attorneys, and your own influence. If these experiences are to be constructive and positive, you should develop a conceptual frame of reference about what is happening, what works, and about the consequences that follow various statements. In other words, in the safety of the moment, be more of the observer part of the participant-observer.

3. *Experiment.* Stretch your limits as a witness. Be masterful when you do not have to. Practice the admit–deny, push–pull, and uses of silence and anticipate lines of questions. Now and then, call on the judge as an ally in appropriate situations even if emotionally and substantively you do not need such an alliance to feel in control. Think of these experiments as practice times for a sport, in which you want your stroke and movements to be as close as possible to the real competition.

4. *Hold the moment.* Instead of thinking of this court appearance as a time you got away without harm, keep the mastery and success of being on the witness stand as actively as you can in your memory. Just as some people can use terrific culinary or sexual or business experiences to carry them through uncertain and troubling periods, the smooth gliding through calm courtroom air can serve a similar purpose.

THE MAXIM: *Quiet times on the stand can be used to observe carefully, stretch personal limits, and incorporate successes.*

❄ 52 ❄

The Rumpelstiltskin Principle

THE TERMS WE USE IN ADDRESSING OTHERS ARE indicators of the quality of the relationship. Positive or negative feelings and dominance–submission are evident from these terms. Take, for instance, the difficulty many individuals have in speaking by name to their mothers-in-law and fathers-in-law. Saying "mother" or "father" is not proper because this term does not quite apply. The phrase "Mother Jones" or "Poppa Smith" seems strained. A common resolution is to avoid all labels for a while, instead saying "ah-er" whenever a name is needed. This struggle with a name reflects the ambiguity in the parent-in-law relationship.

The dominance–submission aspect of relationships is visible in physician–patient terms of address. Most patients call their physicians "Doctor." Most physicians call their patients by their first names. No doubt is present about who is in control. This degree of authority may well impede good communication and promote a sense in the patient of being powerless (Fischer & Brodsky, 1978).

Just for that reason, trying to promote a sense of students being powerful and heard, I ask my students to call me "Stan." Many of them do, but undergraduates at the University of Alabama find it hard not calling a professor "Sir" and instead calling him "Stan." In one course, I had asked all of the students to call me Stan. Part way through the first class, a young man raised his hand and asked me a question, addressing me as "Doctor Brodsky."

"Stan, please," I asked him.

"I beg your pardon," he replied.

"Stan," I asked once more.

He stood.

In the same genre, filled with egalitarian fervor when my son Mike was eight and my daughter Rachel six years old, I asked them to call me by my first name. "Okay, Dad, you bet," they replied together. I never asked again.

The courtroom is a setting in which I pay close attention to what I am called. The title and name used can be vehicles for influence and control. Some attorneys begin each question with the witness's name, with emphasis and rising pitch on each first syllable, and then pause, as if they are holding the witness by the front of the shirt. They say, "DOCtor BRODsky" (pause emphatically), "isn't it true, SIR, that you know much less about your work than we have been led to believe?"

It is uncomfortable to be on the receiving end. Everyone who opts for an unlisted phone number or who withholds personal information from strangers at social gatherings understands this intrusion. Furthermore, most witnesses never learn the opposing attorneys' names and have no ready, appropriate reply. To say in response, "Well, counselor, I probably know much less about my work than *I* believe" may be appealingly modest, but the term *counselor* is awkward.

Instead, I recommend the "Rumpelstiltskin principle" (Brodsky & Poythress, 1985). Remember that, in that Grimm's fairy tale, Rumpelstiltskin promised the miller's daughter, who had become queen, that she would not have to surrender her daughter to him if she could discover his name. She did find out his name, to his fury, and kept her daughter. The lesson for us is that in unfolding courtroom tales as well, we should learn the names of all of the courtroom actors: judge and attorneys, in particular, but also anyone else, including the court reporter, with whom we may speak.

Using the attorneys' names in a parallel form of response to questions that begin with our names gives us power. Instead of being linguistically submissive, we can be at least equal. Thus, the above reply would begin with, "Well, Mr. BELIi, I probably know much less . . ." Of course, this parallel construction and use of name is far from a domination of the exchange. It is, however, one piece of a mosaic of taking charge and feeling in control of the affective climate.

Attorneys do not react badly to being called by name. Rumpelstiltskin was upset about it all. He exclaimed that the devil must have told the queen, stomped his right foot so hard that it went in the ground up to his waist, and then grabbed his left foot and tore himself asunder: the poor sport! Attorneys will hardly blink, but they will not have this small unit of language oneupmanship to themselves.

THE MAXIM: *Know the names and faces of the attorneys, judge, and other participants in the courtroom events.*

❧ 53 ❧

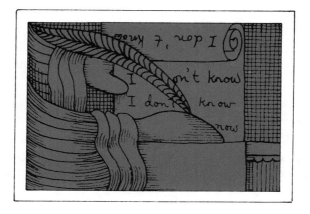

Saying "I Don't Know"

AN EPISODE OF THE TELEVISION SHOW *L.A. LAW* had just begun. While waiting to meet with a potential client, Douglas Brackman, the firm's managing partner, had discovered that other firms making presentations had brought several attorneys along. Brackman started feeling quite alone. His only companion was Bennie, the mildly retarded messenger for the firm who had carried the file boxes. Brackman ordered Bennie to come into the meeting, to pretend he was an attorney, to take notes, and not to say anything. After Brackman finished his presentation, the client asked Bennie what *he* thought. After some hesitation, Bennie replied "I don't know." The client was delighted, saying that was what he wanted and liked, a lawyer who would speak honestly when he did not know something.

So it goes too with court testimony. Witnesses frequently get in trouble by talking about content they do not know.

The stimulus demand of being accepted as expert witnesses is to act expert about everything. The experts are "on stage" and most people are deferential. The experts easily slip into roles of lecturing, explaining, clarifying, pontificating. They feel that all

173

content generally within their areas of professional or scientific knowledge should be given on request.

The consequence is that experts get in serious trouble by talking about topics about which they have only incomplete or obsolete knowledge. They may speak of subjects they studied years ago in school or heard in lectures, without any more current knowledge, or that colleagues have mentioned in passing.

My advice is to learn to say "I don't know" on the witness stand. Good attorneys will discover areas of marginal knowledge, put forth efforts to uncover this marginality, and eventually try to discredit the witness. By saying "I don't know," the witnesses can transform how they are perceived. They can now be seen as having respect for their limitations, having humility, and having the good sense not to trying to know everything in every situation.

The first time a witness says "I don't know," an interesting change takes place in the courtroom. Observers and jury and judge seem to pay attention more closely. The very next statement is heard more vividly. The limits of knowledge are delineated.

Witnesses do not have to use those very words "I don't know." Sometimes the phrase "that's beyond the limits of my expertise" serves well. Alternately, the witnesses may choose to say, "That question really calls for a neuropsychologist to answer it."

A psychological barrier can impede using the statement "I don't know." The barrier is the fear of looking bad, of appearing inexpert. This barrier is so formidable that witnesses need to practice dozens of times saying "I don't know," so that the expression flows effortlessly and syntonically.

When should one avoid saying "I don't know"? The expression should not be used as a gimmick to avoid a stressful interchange, nor should it used as a mock expression of professional modesty. Instead, the statement should be used only when it directly and clearly applies. Under those circumstances, "I don't know" can be a wise and powerful response to a difficult cross-examination question.

174

THE MAXIM: *When you truly do not know, say so.*

✤ 54 ✤

Scientist Challenges

CROSS-EXAMINATION QUESTIONS ABOUT THE EXPERT MENTAL HEALTH witness as scientist seem to go in two opposite directions. In one direction is what I have come to think of as the "teeming masses" inquiry, in which the attorney portrays the professional field as a teeming mass of individual, unrelated opinions and the witness is portrayed as having just one more single, isolated view. The opposite direction is the "esteemed scientific standards" inquiry, in which the cross-examining attorney elicits a description of the purest, best, ideal standards of science and practice compared with which the witness's own work is the essence of mediocrity. I begin with the teeming masses approach and draw from an example by Harold Liebenson (1956) in his book, *The Doctor in Personal Injury Cases.*

> *Q.* "Doctor, is medical science an exact science?"
>
> *A.* "No, it is not an exact science. [If the doctor says it is, he leaves himself open to many questions to disprove this statement.]
>
> *Q.* "It is not unusual for men in the same field to differ in their diagnoses, is it?

A. "No, it is not unusual for such a thing to occur.

Q. "When you gave us your diagnosis, it was your opinion as to the patient's injury, wasn't it?

A. "Yes, sir." (p. 107)

This line of questions may proceed to queries about how supervisors and professors had opinions at times that differed from those of the witness and to the interesting issue of how different clinicians may legitimately ask quite different questions and legitimately come up with quite different answers just for that reason. The attorney's intent sometimes is to have the witness validate the worth of other witnesses' opinions. In the case of prosecution cross-examinations in criminal responsibility trials or defense cross-examinations in personal-injury cases, these questions are planned to suggest that all expert testimony should be disregarded because it is not consistent.

Some ways of handling such cross-examinations have already been noted in the discussion of examiner effects. However, each of the sample questions just listed lends itself to an answer that puts the witness more in control. To the first question of whether medical science is an exact science, the witness might put the question in the broader context of how no sciences are truly exact. When answering a question of this sort, I once discussed how my sister does spectrographic research with collagens and how her scientific work involves much human judgment and interpretation. Thus, it was not that psychology was wishy-washy and uncertain but that some human elements are found in all scientific endeavors.

The second question seeking my confirmation about whether "men in the same field differ in their diagnoses" may be answered with, "Men and women may differ in their diagnoses, but in my experience, it is much more common to find substantial agreement about symptoms, dynamics, and degree of impairment."

The last question, that it was my opinion that I was offering, calls for an affirmative, strong answer that it is indeed my professional opinion based on all of the clinical work I had performed in this case, as well as based on my ten years of experience with these kinds of clients.

The esteemed scientific standards line of questions juxtaposes theoretical levels of high achievement with actual practices by the witnesses. Thus, witnesses may be confronted with the theoretically possible perfect levels of reliability, validity, or perfectly applicable norms and then asked to compare their paltry or, more likely, uncertain levels of accuracy. My outlook is that this comparative information is useful for judges and juries to have and that witnesses should be prepared to share such information openly and nondefensively. However, in this process of sharing professional limitations, effective witnesses should patiently distinguish between esteemed, theoretical scientific standards and practical, accepted standards of practice. The reality of professional practice should be communicated, namely that no practitioners are perfect but that a sound, meaningful, and generalizable base of knowledge does exist on which professional judgments are based.

THE MAXIM: *Both the teeming masses and esteemed scientific standards cross-examinations should be met with a comfortable affirmation of accepted and meaningful standards of practice.*

❧ 55 ❧

The Star-Witness Fantasy

THE RUSTLING OF PAPERS HAS CEASED. BACKGROUND CONVERSATIONS diminish. The court reporter looks expectantly at you, ready to enter every word into what may be a permanent and official record. Every one of your statements is carefully attended to, with the potential for each being challenged. Furthermore, you feel that you are a crucial part of something truly important, not garden-variety important like everyday work, but an event on which a person's freedom or life-long financial well-being may depend. Courtroom appearances can be seen as being so significant that some witnesses have recurring dreams preceding and following their testimony.

Alan Tuckman (1989) has labeled the sense of exaggerated self-importance of the witness as the "star-witness fantasy." In this fantasy, the witness comes to believe that his or her testimony, findings, and personal persuasiveness will either make or break the case. This fantasy arises not only from concentrated attention to the actual testimony in the courtroom but also from the structure of trial evidence. Because evidence must be uncontaminated, the witnesses are discouraged from knowing the other elements of the attorney's case (to say "discouraged" is to say the least—cases or verdicts may be thrown out if witnesses' testimony is tainted with others' knowledge). This requisite insulation can intensify the tendency of some witnesses to think that their testimony and role are the wellspring from which all else flows.

Having the star-witness fantasy causes problems. To begin with, it may make the witness more anxious. If you are the star performer, with most other actors in supporting roles, you had darned well better give a great performance.

A second problem is something that Tuckman (1989) described as "a component of countertransference." What I interpreted this as meaning is that the witness caught up in this fantasy is bringing along an unrealistic, personal agenda, which has elements of self-aggrandizement. The more you are caught up in such personal agendas, the less you are able to be fully present and emotionally stable in a courtroom appearance. Thus, witnesses who are aggressively confronted and scrutinized during cross-examination are more likely to be self-assured and forceful if the witnesses do not feel that their self-esteem and the disposition of the entire trial are at stake.

What to do about this fantasy of being the star witness around whom the case revolves? Diagnosis goes a long way toward a cure. If this process is recognized, some perspective and distance can be attained. Tuckman (1989) urged that witnesses recognize the voluminous nature of the content from which the verdict will be drawn and he suggested sitting in throughout a trial, including summations. Then, Tuckman concluded, "you will truly understand that you are only a small cog in a multifaceted and complex process" (p. 64).

THE MAXIM: *A witness's self-centeredness about the importance of personal testimony can serve as blinders that interfere with clarity, self-assurance, and nondefensiveness.*

❧ 56 ❧

Termination of Parental Rights

O F ALL MENTAL HEALTH LEGAL PROCEDURES, TERMINATION OF parental rights and child custody decisions probably produce the most heat and greatest hazards for the professionals doing the assessments. In wake of the loss of their children, some parents become red-faced infuriated or cold-steel vindictive toward the mental health professionals involved. Colleagues who specialize in this work have at least one horror story to tell. Suits have been filed against them for malpractice. Complaints have been entered with state ethics committees or licensing boards. Harassing telephone calls and threats have been made. Parents who cannot emotionally accept the court's decision seek scapegoats elsewhere, sometimes with unstinting bitterness.

No approach to courtroom testimony can prevent some recriminations. However, general guidelines for such evaluations do exist, and my sample questions will highlight typical cross-examination concerns. Many good sources are available for considering issues in termination of parental rights. I recommend the chapter by psychiatrist Diane Schetky and attorney David Slader in the 1980 book, *Child Psychiatry and the Law*. Termination hearings themselves are highly variable in frequency and nature from state to state. In Oregon, for example, such hearings are common for children in extended foster care, whereas in other states such hearings are rare.

The following cross-examination questions offer a representative sampling of the more difficult issues raised.

"Isn't it true, Doctor, that despite the difficulties you have described, that Mary has a close emotional tie to her mother?" [Yes.] "An isn't it true that breaking of such a close emotional bond, even with a most imperfect mother, can be harmful to the emotional future of a child?"

A good response here addresses the complexity of termination recommendations. The breaking of a tie may certainly be harmful; to Schetky and Slader (1980), keeping a conflicted existing tie interferes with future attachments. Breaking the tie is, however, often seen as less detrimental than the pathological or abusive elements in the relationship.

"You have testified earlier that Mr. A. is episodically able to meet his child's needs. Please describe what a skilled clinician or program of instruction in parenting might do to make such episodes of good parenting more frequent."

This interesting question calls for a program or treatment description. Such an answer belongs to the court for consideration. At the same time, the witness should consider discussing the parent's life-long family relationships (typically quite poor), adequacy in interpersonal relationships, and prognosis and motivation for change. If the prognosis is poor, the court should know that as well.

"Isn't it true that both literature reviews and longitudinal research studies have shown that as many as one fourth of children taken away from their parents and placed apparently permanently in foster homes can be successfully placed back in the parents' home?"

This kind of question should best be met with specific knowledge. The question was drawn from a study summarized in Schetky and Slader (1980), who also noted that the parental re-placement did not work out as well as other placements. A good response would be to discuss this or other relevant studies, demonstrating knowledge and consideration of these issues. Alternatively, suggestions given elsewhere in this book could be used here. The witness might answer that in this individual child's case, he clearly no longer belonged in this home with neglectful and nonempathic parents. The witness could point out that he or she is not familiar with such studies, that the witness is testifying as a clinician, not a researcher, and that the recommendation is based on a clinical evaluation.

THE MAXIM: *The heated emotionality of termination of parental rights hearings calls for exceptionally well-prepared and constructive testimony.*

✤ 57 ✤

Transformative Moments

VIVID EXCHANGES BETWEEN ATTORNEYS AND WITNESSES CAN substantially change the acceptance and meaning of the testimony as well as the entire atmosphere of the courtroom. I have come to think of these exchanges as "transformative moments" because they so quickly influence perceptions, beliefs, and feelings of the courtroom actors. These transformations can be initiated by an attorney, witness, or judge and less often by a defendant, plaintiff, or observer. Television and movie courtroom dramas use transformative moments all of the time. In real life they are infrequent (and certainly less frequent than the continuing bouts of revelation and unsettling confrontation in television shows). Attorneys sometimes plan with care for such moments, saving a particular topic for exactly the right time to leverage the court's opinions.

Expert witnesses can produce negative transformations by self-contradictions, visible uncertainty, and emotional and intellectual distress. Credibility can vaporize with the speed of a cheap perfume. However, my interest is more in positive transformative moments. It is hard to give directions for producing them because on the part of witnesses, they are almost always unplanned and spontaneous. Knowing when they have happened is easy; in one case, I replied to a question with an answer that so cut to the heart of the basic issues that the attorney stammered, stopped, stammered again, stopped, began to ask another question, and in the middle, sat down without another word. Largely because the attorney had been pushy and hostile, I took pleasure at seeing him transmogrified.

Stuart Greenberg, a forensic psychologist in Seattle, wrote to me about such a transformative moment (personal communication, April 19, 1990). My introduction to his case came about because I had told Stu that an opposing counsel on a case coming to trial in Alaska had called me. The attorney had inquired whether Stu had in truth written two articles, with me as co-author, as listed on his résumé. Here is Stu Greenberg's description of what happened.

> At the start of cross-examination, I was quite nervous about what personal impeachment attack was about to be launched. Direct had gone reasonably well and it was evident that he had to try something because the jury had been quite receptive to my discussion of this plaintiff having PTSD [posttraumatic stress disorder] due to having been raped by his client. Thanks to your phone call, I had brought with me copies of the two articles. Cross-exam proceeded like this after a few preliminary questions.
>
> Q: "Dr. Greenberg, according to your vitae, you have published two articles with Dr. Stanley Brodsky?"
>
> A: "Yes, that's correct."
>
> Q: "And one of these articles was published by the Washington State Bar Association in their Bar Journal?"
>
> A: "Yes, that's correct."
>
> Q: "My office called the Bar Association and tried to get a copy of your article from them and they said that they didn't have such a publication. Could you explain why they might have said that?"
>
> A: "No, I can't explain why they might

186

have said that, but I brought a photocopy of the article with me if you would like to see it."

Q: "Yes, please."

A: [Witness hands counsel paper.]

Q: [Counsel leafing through paper] "Dr. Greenberg, this seems to be an article on how to testify in court."

A: "No, actually it's an article written for defense counsel on how to cross-examine mental health experts."

The Court: [Straight-faced but tongue in cheek] "Perhaps counsel would like a few minutes to read the article before proceeding with Dr. Greenberg?"

Everyone in the courtroom cracked up and much to his credit, defense counsel laughed at himself along with everyone else . . . he went on questioning me about the substantial issues in the case and gave me a very good cross examination, something I complimented him on when we were done. He returned the compliment.

All in all it was a fun and satisfying day. The jury subsequently found against his client for $103,000. I'm starting to believe pretty strongly that in the great cosmic scheme of things, life actually is fair.

This transformative moment had several elements worth noting. Humor was involved. The entire courtroom joined in the laughter. The effort to embarrass the witness backfired. And the incident stayed with clarity in the mind of the witness and probably the attorney, judge, and jury. Even though such moments cannot be planned, knowing what they are and how they function in the courtroom can allow witnesses to be alert for opportunities to momentarily transform the courtroom milieu.

THE MAXIM: *Key moments can positively and negatively transform the credibility and acceptance of testimony.*

❧ 58 ❧

The Well-Dressed Witness

AMONG THE MOST FREQUENT QUESTIONS I AM ASKED at expert witness workshops is, "What should I wear?" This question is often followed by descriptions of what clothing attorneys have told the individuals to wear. Dress in earth colors, they have been told, because the jurors will see you as a warmer person. Never wear colored shirts or blouses, some witnesses have been advised by attorneys, because then you appear less serious. Do not ever testify wearing slacks or pants suits, women are sometimes told, because you will seem too masculine. Most such advice is nonsense based on ideas picked up from Sunday supplements and dress-for-success paperbacks and from anecdotes passed from attorney to attorney.

The true difficulty arises when individual witnesses dress and act in ways that are not comfortable and natural for them. My personal experience was with my courtroom suit. This suit was plain black, conservatively cut, made of a wool blend, and worn with white shirts, simple striped ties, and black dress shoes. I wore this suit only to testify in court and for funerals.

Nothing was wrong with the courtroom suit, except that it was not me. I normally wear tweed sports jackets, open-neck shirts, and slip-on or hush puppy shoes in my "dressy" professional appearance. When I wore the courtroom suit, I felt less at home and had to strain to allow myself to be at ease. The necktie seemed to be choking me. The suit felt like a costume.

My first change was to wear sports jackets with ties. I gave the black suit away to a rummage sale. Wearing sports jackets when I testified led to a modest improvement in my acceptance of myself on the witness stand.

The second and far more dramatic change was giving up the necktie. Just about all male participants in trials wear ties and I felt obliged to wear one also. The first time I gave it up was in a trial in Bismarck, North Dakota. A psychiatric patient at the state hospital had jumped off a fourth-floor fire escape in a suicide attempt and was suing the state for not preventing his leap and resulting paraplegia. I was testifying for the State of North Dakota that all reasonable precautions had been taken, given the man's history. I brought a tie, neatly folded in a manila folder, with me to the witness stand, thinking that the tie was a form of security.

I did fine in the testimony. In the corridor afterward, I was asked by the plaintiff's attorney what was in my manila folder.

"It was a necktie," I explained, "just in case I needed it."

"Ah-hah, I should have asked you why you didn't have enough respect for the courts of North Dakota to wear a tie," the attorney exclaimed.

"And I would have replied," I told him, "that I had been so impressed with the warmth and hospitality of the people of North Dakota that I felt comfortable testifying in the clothes I usually wear in my professional work."

Since then I have testified without neckties. No judge or attorney has ever said anything critical. The only observable difference has been my own greater ease.

The instructive lesson in this anecdote is that expert witnesses should dress in a manner that feels professionally appropriate for their normal dressier work. Instead of dressing to conform to a global formula, witnesses should dress to maximize their feelings of esteem and comfort. My discarded courtroom suit would be excellent for some other witnesses. Some women I know wear carefully tailored, severely cut suits with frilly blouses to communicate both professionalism and femininity. The entire range of choices of colors, fabrics, degree of formality, and shoes should follow the person rather than try to lead the person.

However, are there times witnesses should dress in clothing that is not their typical style? Yes. For novice or infrequent witnesses, clothing that offers personal security may be useful. To the degree that clothing reassures the witnesses that they are doing well and being professional, dressing more formally may be helpful. As time goes by, one's sense of security should arise more from within rather than from special clothing designed to evoke particular perceptions.

THE MAXIM: *Dress for court in clothes that are familiar, comfortable, and professional.*

❧ 59 ❧

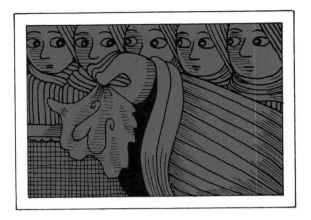

When It Is Over

THE PRINCIPLE OF "RECENCY" IN LEARNING THEORY STATES that the
most recent information a person acquires is retained especially
well. In the case of court testimony, the recency principle translates
into advice to be poised, careful, and confident as you leave the
witness stand.

Jurors sometimes assess effectiveness in part by the attitude
of the witness leaving the stand. The witness who leaves dispirited
and defeated, after a difficult cross-examination, is likely to leave
the impression of having lost. Belli and Carlova (1989) advised their
witnesses, "Don't sigh deeply, mop your brow, look dejected, hang
your head, or slink out of the courtroom" (p. 210). Such impressions
can lead the jurors or the judge to think that you were neither
confident nor correct.

Effective witnesses leave the stand as if they have triumphed,
no matter what has transpired. They hold themselves well, walk
deliberately and comfortably, and exit the courtroom with grace and
dignity. The feeling of having triumphed, of course, can be overdone.
Belli and Carlova (1989) have written about witnesses who have
undermined their effectiveness by grinning at spectators, waving at

friends, and, in one particularly bad example, of a witness who clasped his hands together above his head like a victorious boxer.

Less credible witnesses sometimes seem surprised that it is time to leave the stand or are overly eager to get away from the courtroom. When they do leave, they sometime bump into things. One friend of mine stumbled as he stepped down from the stand, had his loose papers fly out of his case folder and scatter all over the floor. He felt undignified crawling about on his knees and picking up his notes and reports.[1] Other experts avoid eye contact with all parties as they leave, an act that makes it appear as if they are aloof or ashamed.

When I leave, I try to maintain uncharacteristically good posture. I briefly glance at jurors, attorneys, judge, audience, bailiff, court reporter, everyone, with as much of a feeling of comfort and mastery as I can muster.

I have one more suggestion, to be used only occasionally, and only if it feels comfortable to the witness. If my testimony, and the cross-examination in particular, has gone on for a long time, I may say something positive to the attorneys as I pass by. Once, at the close of a day of testimony, I stopped at the table of the opposing attorneys, shook hands with them, and said something to the effect of, "Good questions," and "interesting case." The attorneys were hunched over their notes and talking to each other, so my appearance startled them. They stood, and shook hands with me; this brief interchange demonstrated to the jury in nonverbal terms that our antagonism was transitory.

These closing tactics are not for everyone. Yet, if the witness can leave the courtroom with visible control and mastery, the jury receives a positive impression of effectiveness.

---

[1] While this friend was gathering up his scattered papers, the judge kept saying to him, "Pick up the card." Finally, my friend found a printed card that had slipped to the floor with his papers. The card read, "Be careful stepping down from the witness box."

193

The Maxim: *Make the last impression a good one.*

❄ 60 ❄

When Your Attorney Is
Indifferent or Incompetent

WE SHOULD NOT BE SURPRISED THAT ATTORNEYS ARE enormously variable in their skills and commitment to their work. After all, so are psychologists, social workers, physicians, musicians, insurance agents, and members of every other field and profession. Inept and indifferent attorneys do come along. When we work with such attorneys in preparing for court appearances, they can be a major obstacle to effective testimony.

Staff members at public agencies that deal with neglect of children and elderly people run into many indifferent attorneys. The pattern is familiar; the attorneys keep putting off meeting with the witnesses. The attorneys usually tell the witnesses there is no need to be concerned. Often no meetings and only brief telephone conversations will have preceded the case coming to court. Once in court, the witnesses may find they did not know exactly about what they were expected to testify and that no plan was developed of presenting evidence.

The solution is to be assertive with the attorneys by insisting on a meeting and ensuring that you are not expected to testify inappropriately about any issue or conclusions. Attorneys sometimes repeat that everything will be fine, that they know what they are doing, and just to show up on time. My suggestion for handling such attorneys is to keep it simple, strong, and persistent. Here is one example:

Attorney: "Don't be a worry wart. I have the case in hand. We don't have to meet."

Witness: "That's not okay."

A: "Listen, I have had dozens of cases just like this. I'll just see you in court."

W: "That's not okay."

A: "What's the matter with you? Are you panicking?"

W: "It's important that we meet and go over my testimony. It's not okay just to meet in court."

A: "Let's do this; I will call you if we need to meet."

W: "I appreciate that offer, but that's not okay. I can schedule a meeting after working hours the evening before the hearing, and I can come by your office if that would be more convenient."

A: "I guess that will be okay."

Occasionally, attorneys will resist even this assertive approach. In such cases, it is legitimate to escalate from simple insistence to mild threats of dismissing the attorney from the agency or case. That threat brings around some recalcitrant attorneys.

Incompetent attorneys are a different matter. Although they are readily available to meet with witnesses, they are not able to grasp what is involved in the case. One psychologist friend of mine tells of an attorney who never could understand what schizophrenia was, despite twenty hours of telephone and personal discussions. When the case went to court, the attorney was lost. Indeed, the attorney mispronounced the word and never asked the agreed-on questions.

In my own work, I listen carefully to the attorney during the first telephone contact. If the attorney is inept, I then decide whether to stay with the case (assuming that I have chosen to accept the client for substantive reasons) on the basis of whether the attorney is open to learning and is able to learn what he or she needs to know. If the attorney is indeed open and educable, then I proceed. Otherwise, I decline as politely and as early in the case as I can.

Not all witnesses are in a position to decline a case. However, private practitioners and others with choice should use that choice, and, every now and then, check that they are turning down cases to be certain that such distinctions are being made. More than just legal competence needs to be considered in such judgments. Belli and Carlova (1989) offered two additional criteria: "Do you feel comfortable with your lawyer?" and "Can you talk to him?"

When you decide to educate the attorney as part of your plan, the outcome is sometimes good in unexpected ways. Appreciative attorneys often come back to you and refer other attorneys to you. Furthermore, this teaching role allows you to expand the nature of your work and helps you avoid getting stuck in repetitive tasks.

THE MAXIM: *With indifferent attorneys be assertive. With incompetent attorneys, decline the case or educate them.*

❧ 61 ❧

While Lawyers Fuss

THE MOMENT OFTEN ARRIVES WHEN LAWYERS FUSS AND argue before the bench about accepting the witness as an expert or allowing some aspect of the witness's testimony. All other proceedings cease. The attorneys vigorously point to some legal issue of evidence or procedure that may disallow the witness altogether or disallow a crucial component of the testimony. Sometimes these debates take the form of a three-way conversation between the attorneys at their tables and the judge. At other times the exchanges take place at the bench, within easy hearing of the witness.

Some witnesses are drawn into strong emotional investments in these arguments. As they listen to their careful case histories described as "hearsay," they can feel insulted and may feel their public worth as professionals dangling in the balance of the court's decision. Witnesses with high reactivity can experience two harmful consequences of their emotional investment.

First, they may be viewed by the jurors and other courtroom participants as caring greatly about the outcome of the fussing, hoping that "their" attorney will prevail. This visible emotional posture compromises their apparent objectivity and makes it appear as if they are personally as well as substantively affiliated with the side that called them.

The second potentially adverse consequence is what I think of as, "Oh Lord, they found me out." When the judge rules against the admission of the expert, or one element of the testimony, some witnesses are crestfallen. They feel as if they personally have failed, and this sense of failure shows. As a result, what they say next and what they have said before is less credible.

What to do while lawyers fuss? An option is to remain uninvolved. Norman Poythress tells me that he relaxes and looks to the jury with a slight conspiratorial smile, conveying to the jury a personal distance from the whole process as well as the message that both he and the jury have in common that they have to tolerate such protracted, labrynthian matters.

I have an alternative, albeit somewhat idiosyncratic, solution. During these long arguments, I allow myself to leave my body, to slowly rise straight up toward the ceiling of the courtroom, and to fly above the proceedings. I extend my legs straight out behind me and my arms out to the side and effortlessly glide in rectangular patterns above my body and above all of the people sitting there so seriously. I like to think that a Mona Lisa smile comes over my countenance, a slight, enigmatic smile hinting at profoundness of thought and serenity of mind. Although I am interested in the proceedings, my interest is in the geometrical patterns of people sitting, in the theatrical qualities of the gesturing.

No attorneys (at least up until the time I wrote this) have ever, while I was in this out-of-body experience, asked me what I was thinking, which is a disappointment. For a long time I have been ready with a reply: "Sorry, but my mind was elsewhere."

THE MAXIM: *When lawyers fuss, stay uninvolved.*

❧ 62 ❧

Ziskin & Faust
Are Sitting on the Table

FOR MOST MENTAL HEALTH PROFESSIONALS, THE MULTIPLE VOLUMES by Jay Ziskin and David Faust (1988) about cross-examining expert witnesses are serious concerns. Attorneys often use either the major themes or actual questions from these books to challenge witnesses, and seeing those fat Ziskin and Faust books sitting on the attorney's table is enough to produce a hot rush of anxiety in some witnesses. A second relevant component of the Ziskin and Faust writings is their provocative article in *Science* (Faust & Ziskin, 1988), which essentially concluded that the scientific bases of psychiatry and psychology are insufficient to permit practitioners to meet the legal tests of testifying as expert witnesses. This article was so widely publicized that it has leaked into some cross-examinations in its own right. The cross-examinations go like this:

"Do you accept *Science* as the most prestigious and important publication in the general scientific community?"

"Are you familiar with the Faust and Ziskin article in *Science* about the scientific foundations from which psychologists testify in court?"

"Are you aware that they reviewed over 1,400 articles that deal with the research about the kind of testimony you are giving today?"

"Have you personally reviewed 1,400 articles about the kind of testimony you are giving? How many have you personally reviewed?"

"Were you aware that Faust and Ziskin soundly condemned testimony by psychologists and psychiatrists?"

The skilled attorney would either explore the witnesses' ignorance about the review article or use the content to bludgeon the witness into an admission that real doubts exist about the validity of psychological testimony. So, what to do if you are on the witness stand and these questions are asked?

The strongest line of defense is to portray accurately the Faust and Ziskin (1988) review as one-sided and unrepresentative. Faust and Ziskin prepared their major volumes for attorneys to cross-examine mental health experts and not for the purposes of scientific reviews. Their work comes from an advocacy perspective in the guise of scientific objectivity (Brodsky, 1989b). Expert testimony does, or at least should, come from an impartial perspective.

One especially useful response to such questions can be to note that the Faust and Ziskin (1988) arguments do not represent even a respected minority opinion. That phrase, "respected minority," already has a foundation in the law; in malpractice actions, for example, unusual practices, theories, or approaches have to meet the test of whether they represent a respected minority. My reading of the field is that most practitioners or scholars hold an extremely critical view of Ziskin and Faust. On the basis of the anger (in my mind, unjustified and unnecessary) I have heard at conventions and read in journals, it is questionable how respected the Ziskin and Faust minority is. And, I should add, it is a small minority indeed!

A personal note may be in order here. Jay Ziskin is a friend of mine and he is interested not only in helping lawyers cross-examine mental health experts but also in improving the field. Although his reviews are not altogether fair to practicing clinicians, his criticisms have performed an important function. They have helped the field become more accountable in court for its scholarly and research roots. Those of us who testify have a reason to be grateful for the impetus to reconsider the *whats* and *hows* of our work. It can be quite constructive to say this in court. I find that an overview of the field, acknowledging the contributions of Faust and Ziskin and speaking to how we have attended to their issues, disarms attorneys and is part of nondefensive, positive testimony.

THE MAXIM: *The Ziskin and Faust reviews have an adversarial component and consequently may not meet the respected minority test. Nevertheless, they have made us more accountable and that can be acknowledged constructively.*

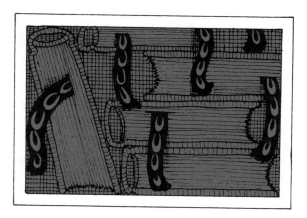

References

Alton, W. G., Jr. (1977). *Malpractice: A trial lawyer's advice for physicians (How to avoid, how to win)*. Boston: Little, Brown.

American Psychiatric Association. (1987). *Diagnostic and statistical manual of mental disorders* (3rd ed., rev.). Washington, DC: Author.

American Psychological Association. (1985). *Standards for educational and psychological testing*. Washington, DC: Author.

American Psychological Association Committee on Children, Youth, and Families and Committee on Psychological Tests and Assessment. (1990). *Statement on the use of anatomically detailed dolls in forensic evaluations.* (Available from the Public Interest Directorate, American Psychological Association, 1200 Seventeenth Street NW, Washington, DC 20036.)

Belli, M. B., Sr., & Carlova, J. (1989). *Belli for your malpractice defense* (2nd ed.). Oradell, NJ: Medical Economics Books.

Boat, B. W., & Everson, M. D. (1988). Interviewing young children with anatomical dolls. *Child Welfare, 67,* 337–352.

Brodsky, S. L. (1977). The mental health professional on the witness stand: A survival guide. In B. D. Sales (Ed.), *Psychology in the legal process* (pp. 269–276). New York: Spectrum Publications.

Brodsky, S. L. (1989a). Testimony about elder abuse and guardianship. *Journal of Elder Abuse and Neglect, 1*(2), 9–15.

Brodsky, S. L. (1989b). Advocacy in the guise of scientific objectivity: An examination of Faust and Ziskin. *Computers in Human Behavior, 5,* 261–264.

Brodsky, S. L., & Poythress, N. G. (1985). Expertise on the witness stand: A practitioner's guide. In C. P. Ewing (Ed.), *Psychology, psychiatry, and the law: A clinical and forensic handbook* (pp. 389–401). Sarasota, FL: Professional Resource Exchange.

Brodsky, S. L., & Robey, A. (1973). On becoming an expert witness: Issues of orientation and effectiveness. *Professional Psychology, 3*, 173–176.

Cooper, E. B., & Cooper, C. S. (1985). *Cooper Personalized Fluency Control Therapy* (rev.). Allen, TX: DLM Teaching Resources.

Curran, W. J., & McGarry, A. L. (1986). The psychiatrist as expert witness. In W. J. Curran, A. L. McGarry, & S. A. Shah (Eds.), *Forensic psychiatry and psychology: Perspectives and standards for interdisciplinary practice.* Philadelphia: F. A. Davis.

Danet, B., & Kermish, N. C. (1978). Courtroom questioning: A sociolinguistic perspective. In L. N. Massery II (Ed.), *Psychology and persuasion in advocacy.* Reno, NV, and Washington, DC: The Association of Trial Lawyers of America, 1978 National College of Advocacy.

Dohrenwend, B. P., & Dohrenwend, B. S. (1974). Social and cultural influences upon psychopathology. *Annual Review of Psychology, 25,* 419–452.

Draguns, J. G. (1982). Methodology in cross-cultural psychopathology. In I. Al-Issa (Ed.), *Culture and psychopathology* (pp. 33–70). Baltimore: University Park Press.

Eissler, K. R. (1986). *Freud as an expert witness: The discussion of war neuroses between Freud and Wagner-Jauregg.* Madison, CT: International Universities Press.

Ekman, P. (1985). *Telling lies: Clues to deceit in the marketplace, politics, and marriage.* New York: Norton.

Equal Employment Opportunity Commission Guidelines. (1990). 29 Code of Federal Register. 1601 *et seq.*

Faust, D., & Ziskin, J. (1988). The expert witness in psychology and psychiatry. *Science, 241,* 31–35.

Fischer, C. T., & Brodsky, S. L. (1978). *Client participation in human services: The Prometheus principle.* New Brunswick, NJ: Transaction.

Goodman, G. S., & Aman, C. (1990). Children's use of anatomically detailed dolls to recount an event. *Child Development, 61,* 1859–1871.

Greenberg, S. A., Feldman, S. R., & Brodsky, S. L. (1987, January). Exposing the experts. *Bar Bulletin,* pp. 23, 28.

Grisso, T. (1981). *Juveniles' waiver of rights: Legal and psychological competence.* New York: Plenum Press.

Grisso, T. (1986). *Evaluating competencies: Forensic assessments and instruments.* New York: Plenum Press.

Grudin, R. (1982). *Time and the art of living.* New York: Ticknor & Fields.

Hill, L. (1989, September 25). Speech therapy helping ambitious execs, young professionals. *Dialogue: Faculty/Staff News* (University of Alabama), p. 1.

Hovey, M. A., & Brodsky, S. L. (1990, December). *Testifying in court about child sexual abuse: Challenges to validity of the investigation and to honesty of the child.* Paper presented at the Florida Department of Law Enforcement Conference on Crimes Against Children, Tampa, FL.

Jampole, L., & Weber, M. K. (1987). An assessment of the behavior of sexually abused and nonsexually abused children with anatomically correct dolls. *Child Abuse and Neglect, 11,* 187–192.

Jones, D., & McGraw, J. (1987). Reliable and fictitious accounts of sexual abuse to children. *Journal of Interpersonal Violence, 2,* 27–45.

Jourard, S. M. (1971). *The transparent self* (2nd ed.). Englewood Cliffs, NJ: Insight.

Kelsey, H. W. (1983). *101 bridge maxims.* Louisville, KY: Devyn Press.

Kurtz, M., & McClung, G. G. (1974). *Care and feeding of witnesses—Expert and otherwise* (Public Employment Practices Bulletin 8). Chicago: International Personnel Management Association.

Lazer, H. A. (1989). This, that, or some other place. *Ottotole, 3,* 82–89.

Liebenson, H. A. (1956). *The doctor in personal injury cases.* Chicago: Year Book Publishers.

Lloyd, R. M. (1989). Zen and the art of contract formation. *Journal of Legal Education, 39,* 185–187.

Macdonald, J. M. (1969). *Psychiatry and the criminal: A guide to psychiatric examinations for the criminal court* (2nd ed.). Springfield. IL: Charles C Thomas.

McClosky, M., & Egeth, H. E. (1983). Eyewitness identification: What can a psychologist tell a jury? *American Psychologist, 38,* 550–563.

McConnell, J. V. (1969). A psychologist looks at the medical profession. In A. G. Sugerman (Ed.), *Examining the medical expert: Lectures and trial demonstrations* (pp. 61–84). Ann Arbor, MI: Institute of Continuing Legal Education.

McDowell, D. (1989). Aging America: The images of abuse. *Journal of Elder Abuse and Neglect, 1*(2), 1–7.

Melton, G. B., Petrila, J., Poythress, N. G., & Slobogin, C. (1987). *Psychological evaluations for the courts: A handbook for mental health professionals and lawyers.* New York: Guilford Press.

Mendelson, G. (1988). *Psychiatric aspects of personal injury claims.* Springfield, IL: Charles C Thomas.

Nordstrom, N., Jr. (1962). *The rights and rewards of the medical witness and medical and dental appraiser.* Springfield, IL: Charles C Thomas.

O'Barr, W. M. (1978). Legal assumptions about language. In L. N. Massery II (Ed.), *Psychology and persuasion in advocacy.* Reno, NV, and Washington, DC: The Association of Trial Lawyers of America, 1978 National College of Advocacy.

207

Poythress, N. G. (1980). Coping on the witness stand: Learned responses to "learned treatises." *Professional Psychology, 11,* 169–179.

Poythress, N. G. (1982). Concerning reform in expert testimony: An open letter from a practicing psychologist. *Law and Human Behavior, 6,* 39–43.

Robinson, D. N. (1980). *Psychology and law: Can justice survive the social sciences?* Oxford, England: Oxford University Press.

Rogers, R. (1984). Toward an empirical model of malingering and deception. *Behavioral Science and the Law, 2,* 93–111.

Rogers, R., Harris, M., & Wasyliw, O. (1983). Observed and self-reported psychotherapy in NGRI acquittees in court mandated outpatient treatment. *International Journal of Offender Therapy and Comparative Criminology, 27,* 143–149.

Rogers, R., Turner, R., Helfield, R., & Dickens, S. (1988). Forensic psychiatrists' and psychologists' understanding of insanity: Misguided expertise? *Canadian Journal of Psychiatry, 33,* 691–695.

Rosenhan, D. L. (1973). On being sane in insane places. *Science, 179,* 250–258.

Sarbin, T. R., & Juhasz, J. B. (1982). The concept of mental illness: A historical perspective. In I. Al-Issa (Ed.), *Culture and psychopathology* (pp. 71–109). Baltimore: University Park Press.

Schetky, D. H., & Slader, D. L. (1980). Termination of parental rights. In D. H. Schetky & E. P. Benedek (Eds.), *Child psychiatry and the law* (pp. 107–118). New York: Brunner/Mazel.

Sivian, A. B., Schor, D. P., Koeppl, G. K., & Noble, L. D. (1988). Interaction of normal children with anatomical dolls. *Child Abuse and Neglect, 12,* 295–304.

Tracy, J. E. (1957). *The doctor as a witness.* Philadelphia: W. B. Saunders.

Tuckman, A. J. (1989). Into the lion's den: Preparation for courtroom testimony. In R. Rosner & R. B. Harmon (Eds.), *Criminal court consultation.* New York: Plenum Press.

White, S., & Santilli, G. (1988). A review of clinical practices and research data on anatomical dolls. *Journal of Interpersonal Violence, 3,* 430–442.

Ziskin, J. (1981). *Coping with psychiatric and psychological testimony* (Vol. 2, 3rd ed.). Venice, CA: Law and Psychology Press.

Ziskin, J., & Faust, D. (1988). *Coping with psychiatric and psychological testimony* (Vols. 1–3, 4th ed.). Marina del Rey, CA: Law and Psychology Press.